AT THE CENTER OF
THE HUMAN DRAMA

The 1991 Michael J. McGivney Lectures
of the John Paul II Institute for Studies
on Marriage and Family

AT THE CENTER OF THE HUMAN DRAMA

The Philosophical Anthropology of
Karol Wojtyła/Pope John Paul II

Kenneth L. Schmitz

with an appendix by John M. Grondelski

The Catholic University of America Press
Washington, D.C.

The paper used in this publication meets the minimum requirements of American
National Standards for Information Science—Permanence of Paper for Printed
Library Materials. ANSI Z39.48-1984.
∞

LIBRARY OF CONGRESS CATALOGING-IN-PUBLICATION DATA
Schmitz, Kenneth L., 1922–
    At the center of the human drama : the philosophical anthropology of Karol
Wojtyła/Pope John Paul II / Kenneth L. Schmitz ; with an appendix by
John M. Grondelski.
        p.   cm. — (Michael J. McGivney lectures of the John Paul II Institute
for Studies on Marriage and Family ; 1991)
    Includes bibliographical references and index.
        1. John Paul II, Pope, 1920–   —Contributions in doctrine of man.
2. Philosophical theology—History—20th century.   3. Man (Christian
theology)—History of doctrines—20th century.   4. Catholic Church—
Doctrines—History—20th century.   I. Title.   II. Series.
B4691.J644S36   1993
128'.092—dc20
93-18202
    ISBN 0-8132-0779-7 (alk. paper). — ISBN 0-8132-0780-0 (pbk. : alk. paper)

Dedicated to His Eminence Bernard Cardinal Law
and to my sometime colleagues at the
Cambridge Center for the Study of Faith
and Culture

Contents

Foreword

The Knights of Columbus are known for their many good works. I can only hope that in a small way this publication is one of them. I am indebted to them and to the Supreme Knight Virgil C. Dechant for the invitation to give the 1991 McGivney Lectures. I owe thanks in a special way to Dr. Carl Anderson, Dean of the John Paul II Institute for Studies on Marriage and Family in Washington, D.C. His encouragement permitted me to set aside—perhaps less important, and certainly less pleasurable—matters in order to prepare the lectures. Over the past three years, the faculty of the Institute has made my visits there an occasion of learning. I am particularly grateful to the Reverend Francis Martin and Professor Stanisław Grygiel for their timely comments, and to the Reverend Romanus Cessario, O.P., and Msgr. Lorenzo Albacete for conversations that helped me along the way. Barbara Carrescia and Teresa Clark have been gracious in anticipating the steps in the preparation and production of the lectures and the original manuscript. The director of the Catholic University of America Press, David McGonagle, Susan Needham and the staff provided expert guidance at every stage in transposing the lectures into the present book.

The hospitality accorded me by the Prior and Treasurer of the community at the Dominican House of Studies in Washington, D.C., the President of the Pontifical Faculty there, and the members of the community has been worthy of St. Thomas Aquinas's commentary on friendship. Among Polish friends I owe particular thanks to Dr. Andrzej Poltawski who sent me German translations of a most helpful sort. I can only hope that I have used them to the benefit of a better understanding of the thought of his countryman. It is with the same end in mind that John Grondelski has kindly appended a bibliography in the hope that additional translations might broaden the understanding of the thought of Karol Wojtyła/John Paul II among English readers. Fr. Jarosław Kupczak, O.P., has helped me with details of Polish expression that lay beyond my own competence.

Many friends and colleagues have contributed to these lectures. The dedication is meant to acknowledge my appreciation of Cardinal Law's support in my early studies of Karol Wojtyła/John Paul II's work. My thanks go out also to my former colleagues at the Cambridge Center for the Study of Faith and Culture: to the president of the Center, Sister Madonna Murphy, C.S.C.; to the Right Reverend Francis George, O.M.I., now bishop of Yakima; to Monsignor Richard Malone, the Reverend Dariusz Slezsynski, the Reverend Stephen DiGiovanni, and Clare Coleman. Learning is sweetened by friendship, and scholarship is eased by community. I owe thanks, too, to the members of the Oblate House in Brighton, Massachusetts, for providing me with an intermittent home away from home during the two years at the Center and for their companionship.

The list is long, yet still incomplete and flawed, were I not to acknowledge my gratitude to my dearest friend and spouse of many years, Lillian, who gave me intelligent and enthusiastic support, and who saw that the many things that would have been left undone were done, as the spirit of the enterprise grew upon me.

Toronto
February 1993

CHAPTER ONE

On Stage
New Words for Ancient Truths

The present pope has caught the imagination of many throughout the world—Christians or not. And he has done it by playing out the drama inherent in the world's oldest elective office, often in new ways. From the Chair of Peter he has poured his energies above all into the task of universal teacher, the voice at the center of the Catholic Church; his actions for the most part flow out of that teaching. It has been his intention to build up the Church from within, by word and deed; but it is clearly also his hope to stand with Christ at the center of the events that shape all mankind. The formative elements of his instruction and action can be traced as they have grown out of the intuitions of a rather remarkable young man from Wadowice. I purpose in these lectures to sketch some of those elements and that formation—simplifying by necessity, if not out of ignorance, but attempting to stay near the main lines of development, especially with regard to his philosophical ideas. For they have articulated his religious sensibilities and contributed to his theological reflections.

Although the central intuitions matured in their proper time, they seem already to have received a certain shape and impetus when in 1939 the young Karol Wojtyła set about his higher studies at the Jagiellonian University—Copernicus's university—in Cracow. For he took up the study of Polish letters, language, and history. As you know, the period 1940–45 coincided with some of the darkest years of that nation's dark yet glorious history. Wojtyła's interest leaned toward the record of that history as it was given expression by poets and national heroes. The dramatic energy of his later works and deeds no doubt found early expression in this interest. He did not fail to notice the interplay of word and deed in that national record. But his religious interest was caught also by an older history—biblical history. His first works for the theater gave dramatic expression to the blending of themes played out in those different histories. In these first dramatic works and in a time of great national suffering, he forged a convergence that deliberately overrode the difference in times between the events in ancient Israel, those in Poland's past, and the terrible events during the dreadful Nazi occupation.

A first play, no longer extant, was entitled *David.*[1] The second (Spring 1940) took up the theme of *Job,* and the third (Summer 1940) that of *Jeremiah,* sub-titled *A National Drama in Three Acts.* I have the impression that in Polish culture, as in some other cultures, more perhaps than in our own, the word has a special weight. It may be the particular genius of the language, or because the language was the last bastion the nation could fall back upon in defense of its cultural identity—I do not know. What is certain, at any rate, is that the young Wojtyła was fascinated by the word— spoken, written, and declaimed. Less than a month after the end of hostilities and the beginning of the occupation of his native land, he wrote to a fellow thespian: "Let theater be a church where the national spirit will flourish."[2]

Wojtyła worked at this time in a quarry (and later in a chemical plant) while he pursued his university studies covertly. During this time he joined forces with Mieczysław Kotlarczyk in a clandestine theater of the "living word." Gathered in cramped domestic quarters in the sparse conditions of occupied Poland, the Rhapsodic Theater Company (as it came to be known) produced seven plays during the years 1941 to 1944, gave twenty-two performances, and held over a hundred rehearsals under the most dangerous conditions. Of this time, Wojtyła was later to remark: "Of all the

---

1. For a more detailed discussion of Wojtyła's early theatrical activity—as dogsbody, actor, prompter, director, playwright—and his continuing interest in the theater, see the introduction by Bolesław Taborski (ed.) in Karol Wojtyła, *The Collected Plays and Writings on Theater* (Berkeley: U of California Press, 1987), pp. 1–16; hereafter, *CP.*

2. Quoted by Taborski, in *CP*, p. 5, from a letter of the nineteen-year-old Wojtyła to Mieczysław Kotlarczyk, written on Nov. 2, 1939, in which he urged Kotlarczyk to come to Cracow in order to form a theater company.

complex resources of the theatrical art, there remained only the living word, spoken by people in extrascenic conditions, in a room with a piano. That unheard-of-scarcity of the means of expression turned into a creative experiment."[3]

A theater critic has referred to the Rhapsodic Theater as "a theater of the imagination, a theater of the inner self."[4] Even after the war, Wojtyła's own plays continued to employ severe staging, symbolic background music and dance, and a chorus that gives emphasis to the ethical implications at decisive points;[5] but all of these extra-verbal accoutrements are subordinated to the inner discipline of the word and its meaning. Indeed, he distinguishes the theater of the word from more traditional theater by the different roles played out by the word in each: "The position of the word in a theater is not always the same. As in life, the word can appear as an integral part of action, movement, and gesture, inseparable from all human practical activity; or it can appear as 'song'—separate, independent, intended only to contain and express thought, to embrace and transmit a vision of the mind."[6]

In traditional theater, the word accompanies the other elements which surround it as part of the total theatrical action, whereas in the theater of the word it is the word that frames the whole. And it is the word that draws out of its own meaning whatever movement, gesture, and background complements its expression. That is why, as far as possible, the staging and music, and every gesture of actor, chorus or dance group, turns upon and synchronically with the turn of the words. Whereas traditional theater tells a story through the impact of event upon character, the theater of the word

3. "Drama of Word and Gesture" (1957) (CP, p. 379).
4. Maria Bojarska, a contemporary drama critic; cited by Taborski, CP, p. 7— In The Jeweler's Shop (1960), act 3, scene 4 (CP, p. 316), Monica imagines her forthcoming wedding day "like rehearsals in a theater: the theater of my imagination and the theater of my thought."
5. In "Rhapsodies of the Millenium" (1958) (CP, p. 386), Wojtyła remarks: "The Rhapsodic Theater asks young actors to subordinate themselves to the great poetic word. This can be felt particularly when the word is developed in immaculately spoken choruses. A group of people collectively, somehow unanimously, subordinated to the great poetic word, evoke ethical associations; this solidarity of people in the word reveals particularly strongly and accentuates the reverence that is the point of departure for the rhapsodists' work and the secret of their style."
6. "On the Theater of the Word" (1952) (CP, p. 372).

sets forth a problem, an issue of import: "The problem itself acts,
rouses interest, disturbs, evokes the audience's participation, demands understanding and a solution."[7] The word and its meaning
"mature in spare, simple, rhythmic gesture," and the movement,
sounds, and staging arise out of the reservoir of meaning contained
in the words and in the problem they articulate. To be sure, the
drama of the word is frankly intellectual: "The new proportions
between word and movement, between word and gesture, doubt-
less reach even further, in a sense beyond theater and into the
philosophical concept of man and the world. The supremacy of
word over gesture indirectly restores the supremacy of thought
over movement and impulse in man."[8]

Such a theatrical presentation is not static, however, but moves
rather with the dynamics of thought, and with the dynamics of the
issue at stake, which "the living human word grasps and makes
into a nucleus of action." The theater of the word, he tells us,
"does not infringe on the realist standpoint but enables us to
understand the inner base of human action, the very fulcrum of
human movement."[9] Such inner dramas must draw upon concrete
and relevant issues and refer them to the world of thought—and
he underscores the last word: not fantasy but thought.[10] Indeed,
in his last play, *Radiation of Fatherhood* (1964), which he subtitles
A Mystery, the figure of the mother says: "At no point can the
world be fiction, the inner world even less than the external world.
. . . It is no metaphor, but reality (that is played out on stage). The
world cannot depend on metaphor alone, the inner world even less
than the external world."[11] And so the theater of the word aims

7. Ibid. (*CP*, p. 373).
8. In "Drama of Word and Gesture" (*CP*, pp. 380–82), Wojtyła further insists
that in the theater of the word, while the word is freed from externals to a large
degree, it must not be divorced from thought, since thought provides the basis for
the unique theatrical realism of the theater of the word.—In "On the Theater of
the Word," no. 2 (*CP*, p. 375), he is careful, moreover, to distinguish the deeper
symbolic realism of the theater of the word from the surface realism of naturalism.
9. "Drama of Word and Gesture" (*CP*, p. 380).
10. In "Rhapsodies of the Millenium" (1958) (*CP*, p. 383), he insists that the
Rhapsodists "not only derive the word from the immediate needs of concrete life
but also refer to that life from the world of thought. Not—it must be stressed—
the world of fantasy, but the world of thought."
11. *Radiation*, part 1, scene 5 (*CP*, p. 341). She affirms that, as the radiation

at being a theater of reality—if I may so put it—at "symbolic realism."

By slowing the pace of the action and reducing the external surroundings, such a drama intends to effect a catharsis, as all drama must; it is a catharsis not primarily of feeling, however, but of meaning. And indeed, at their best, Wojtyła's own dramas reach high dramatic effects. Paradoxically, such a reduced external structure permits the dramatic presentation of themes too broad for a traditional stage, even though the traditional stage is physically more spacious than the setting of the theater of the word. The traditional stage achieves marvellous effects in its own way, but it is bound inextricably to the particularities of its setting and plot, so that it proves too narrow to do justice to the large, even eternal, themes that only a drama of thought can embrace with the freedom adequate to their treatment.[12]

Let us select several themes that are prominent in the dramas and important to my purpose. There can be no doubt that *Job* was composed in the first anguish of a brutal occupation, yet the script of the drama remains faithful in substance to the biblical text as its subtitle declares: *A Drama from the Old Testament*. The inscription on the title page forges the convergence of past, present, and future times under the eternal word of God:

The Action Took Place in the Old Testament Before Christ's Coming. The Action Takes Place in Our Days In Job's Time For Poland and the World. The Action Takes Place in the Time of Expectation, Of Imploring Judgment, In the Time of Longing For Christ's Testament, Worked Out In Poland's and the World's Suffering.[13]

---

of the Fatherhood of God, creation is neither fiction nor metaphor. The primacy of truth as normative principle of reality recurs throughout the plays; but also the caution not to separate truth from love.

12. In "Drama of Word and Gesture" (*CP*, p. 382), he remarks: "The word, however, must not be divorced from thought. The specific base of theatrical realism discovered by Mieczysław Kotlarczyk with his company opens wide the horizons of theatrical practice to encompass works that by their nature could not otherwise be the object of theatrical production. . . . Perhaps other great works of the human mind, for instance the works of philosophers, could thus be adapted for at least some audiences."

13. *Job*, title page (*CP*, p. 25).—Already in a letter of Nov. 2, 1939, to Kot-

No doubt, then, that Poland is borne in mind as a collective Job. The Epilogue repeats what the Prologue chants: "Behold, my people—and listen to the Word of the Lord, you who are downtrodden, you who are flogged, sent to the camps, you—Jobs—Jobs."[14] At the point in the biblical text, however, at which Elihu enters (Job 32), the close adherence to the biblical text breaks off. With the conclusion of the argument between Job and his erstwhile friends, the young man Elihu is seized with the spirit of prophecy and the drama turns to the vision of the coming of Christ, His passion and death: "He is coming—I know He lives. . . . I see that the Redeemer lives."[15] In place of the speeches of Yahweh in the biblical text, we hear a Voice which can be none other than that of Christ in the Garden of Gethsemane. And with that, suffering takes on a positive inner meaning.[16] As the first light of a new dawn begins to break behind the stage curtain, Elihu promises that a New Covenant shall arise from the Suffering. And the drama comes to a close with the counsel:

Take these words against the storm; hold them when darkness descends. They will be for you like the silent lightning cutting the sky above Job. . . . Thus God's waves wash over us, overthrowing one, raising up another. Watch the waves—watch the waves. Nourish your heart today, brother. This is a tragedy of suffering—the sacrificial circle is closed. Depart—with a song on your lips. Depart from here—remember.[17]

ᕳ

In the next drama, *Jeremiah*, the connection with Polish history is made even more explicit.[18] It is ostensibly set amid the great

larczyk, Wojtyła had written: "I think that our liberation ought to be a gate for Christ. I think of an Athenian Poland, but more perfect than Athens with all the magnitude of Christianity, such as our great poets imagined, those prophets of Babylonian captivity" (quoted by Taborski, in *CP*, p. 75).—For some details of the occupation, as well as later events, see the personal memoir of a friend: M. Maliński, *Pope John Paul II. The Life of Karol Wojtyła*. trans. P. S. Falla (New York: Crossroad, 1981).

14. *Job*, "Prologos" (*CP*, p. 29); repeated in "Epilogos" (*CP*, p. 72).

15. *Job* (*CP*, p. 68).

16. Cf. the apostolic letter *Salvifici Dolores: On the Christian Meaning of Human Suffering* (11 Feb. 1984; Vatican trans., Boston: Daughters of St. Paul).

17. *Job*, "Epilogos" (*CP*, p. 73).

18. For helpful details regarding the historical figures and situation see Taborski, *CP*, pp. 75–91.

events of the seventeenth century, but it also resonates with the
Poland of 1940 and with Jeremiah's plaint: "The city has fallen.
. . . The enemies have struck Judah. . . . For the temples of Zion
have been entered by the unclean band of armed heathen."[19] The
theme of the primacy of truth is once again played out. We learn
that to be chosen by God means to be "chosen to proclaim God's
truth." And, following upon the playing of the *Miserere* (Psalm
51), Jeremiah's cry is surely heard against the propaganda that
filled the airwaves of 1940: "One must throw truth across the path
of lies. One must throw truth into the eye of a lie."[20] For "in truth
are freedom and excellence," but in untruth, only slavery.

And yet for all the importance attached to words, the seventeenth-century Jesuit priest, Father Peter Skarga Paweski, warns
that "words are not enough, not enough"; he continues: "One
must catch hearts to kindle them, furrow hearts as with a plough,
and root up the weeds—root them out."[21] The crown Hetman,
Stanisław Żółkiewski, adds, "At the feet of truth one must erect
love; at the foundations, low in the ground, it will take root even
in a wilderness, will build, uplift, and transform all things."[22]

∾

The postwar plays intensify and deepen the religious theme. The
accent is even more consciously upon the "inner space" of the
drama. The path within is meant to search out the truth about
humanity in the maze of Stalinist realism with its clichés, and beyond that, to touch upon the central character's "spiritual strug-

19. *Jeremiah*, act 3: "The Lamentations of Jeremiah" (*CP*, p. 130), broadly
paraphrased in the drama after the fashion of monastic chant.
20. *Jeremiah*, act 1 (*CP*, pp. 101–3, 109).
21. *Jeremiah*, act 1 (*CP*, p. 98); act 2 (*CP*, p. 121).
22. *Jeremiah*, act 2 (*CP*, p. 121), adding: "In your speeches you call for
truth. . . ." To which Father Peter replies: "A call of despair is in my speeches.
Mine is not a voice of revelation. . . ." This is a reference to Father Peter's jeremiad
against the injustices of his day and the prophecy that Poland would fall because
of them. In act 3 (*CP*, p. 137), he warns: "The ship sways but still sails on im-
pressively," but "worms already hatching, though, eat her from within." And yet
the drama sounds a note of hope. The Hetman speaks (*CP*, p. 138): "What is
beyond is God's. There man will not dare. One man cannot sway the hearts of a
people. He can sow the seed, graft a seedling, but does the plant grow as man wills
it to grow? It grows as God wills, for God's is the harvest."

gles and his progress to sanctity."²³ Wojtyła tells us, however, that the intention is not to recount the psychological experiences of the characters but to follow up a line that is "inaccessible to history . . . an extrahistorical element in man lies at the very sources of his humanity."²⁴

The third extant play, *Our God's Brother* (1945–50; published in 1979, first staged in 1980), is a study of Adam Chmielowski (1845–1916), a partisan fighter and an artist, who later as Brother Albert worked with the poor of Cracow and founded congregations of religious brothers and sisters dedicated to that work.²⁵ The forces of the drama swirl about and within Adam.

A major topic of conversation in the circle around Adam addresses the question of the social responsibility of art. A colleague protests against subjectivism in art because it betrays the true nature of artistic creation: "For in reality something slowly grows around you (during the process of artistic creation), gathers momentum, widens. Of course, though you have a part in it, you are not the only originator of this mystery. That much is clear." And indeed, some of the circle consider Adam to be a seeker who is drawn out of himself.²⁶ Adam remains unconvinced, however, at least as it applies to his own artistic work. Instead, he sees his

23. Comment by Taborski, *CP*, p. 152.—In his own introduction to *Our God's Brother*, Wojtyła remarks (*CP*, p. 159) that "this will be an attempt to penetrate the man . . . the fact of humanity—and concrete humanity at that."

24. From Wojtyła's own introduction to *Our God's Brother* (*CP*, p. 159). This does not mean that one abstracts from the historical situation of the characters, but only that a human being is not exclusively historical. In this search, one arrives at probability: "Probability, however, is always an expression of the truth one has searched for; what matters is how much real truth it contains. And that depends on the intensity and integrity of the search." The aim is "to participate in the same multifarious reality in which [the character] participated—and in a way similar to him."—In *Forefathers' Eve and the Twentieth Anniversary* (1961), referring to the Rhapsodic Theater, Wojtyła insists that the drama's inwardness is not an "epic of introspection," and that "the drama does more than analyze [the heroes'] experiences and recreate the stream of their 'dramatic consciousness'" (*CP*, p. 390).

25. He was canonized by the pope in 1983.—For a correlation of the various characters in the drama with Chmielowski and his circle, see Taborski, *CP*, pp. 147–57 and footnotes.

26. *Our God's Brother*, act 1 (*CP*, p. 169): ". . . a typical seeker. Not one who rummages for petty things, but a vigorous, even boisterous seeker."

painting as a means of running away from something or someone indefinable.[27]

Another painter friend, Max, defends subjectivism. He argues that it is sufficient that an artist explore his own selfhood and give it expression; if it interests others, that is beside the point. Max will admit that he has a public persona, but he dubs this public persona "the exchangeable man," since it is subject to the barter of social life. The genuine and inviolable person, he insists, is private; he dubs that persona "the non-exchangeable man," withdrawn behind the fortress façade of an inaccessible loneliness.[28] A fellow artist protests that such an attitude diminishes the meaning of art and its creative power, and the discussion continues.

Adam cannot accept the isolated loneliness advocated by Max, but neither can he be satisfied with the safe routine of social life: "Yes, we are hiding; we escape to little islands of luxury, to the so-called social life, to so-called social structure and feel secure. But no. This security is a big lie, an illusion. It blinds our eyes and stops up our ears, but it will shatter in the end."[29]

Several rather mysterious protagonists enter into the discussion. A principal character is called the Stranger, without further identification; but he seems to represent in some way the revolutionary,

27. ". . . something, or rather someone, in oneself and in all those people" (*Our God's Brother*, act 1 [*CP*, pp. 182–83]). Adam protests that "something in me keeps opening up . . . it's chasing me." It is a painful, "gradual elucidation," which a theologian friend thinks may be a vocation; yet when Adam asks, "To what?" the reply is given, "I don't know. You must keep running away." Cf. Francis Thompson's *The Hound of Heaven*: "I fled Him, down the nights and down the days; / I fled Him, down the arches of the years; / I fled Him, down the labyrinthine ways / Of my own mind. . . ."

28. The theme of loneliness in modern life and the fragmentation of society will recur again and again in Wojtyła's later writings. Cf. *Radiation of Fatherhood* on loneliness and the theme of fragmentation in his social encyclicals.

29. In *Our God's Brother*, act 1 (*CP*, p. 179), Adam remarks: "Each of us goes his own way. Each builds his own nest. Meanwhile, for so many people the road has become too narrow. They have nowhere to stand. They have no patch of ground they can call their own, no slice of bread they can earn, no child they can bring into this world without the certainty that it will be in everybody's way. And in the midst of all this we move, arrogantly confident in the strength of a general system that makes us ignore what cries out to be heard and suppress a justified outbreak."—The whole section resonates with social comment.

who counts on the anger of the poor to break open the circle of poverty in the name of justice denied.[30] Nowhere in the play is there any indication that the playwright disagrees with the justice of this anger, and in several places he has given it eloquent expression through the mouth of the Stranger.[31] Adam rebukes the Stranger for exploiting the just anger of the poor, but he too recognizes the justice of that anger. Going against its grain, however, and in the name of an at-this-point unnamed love, he calls upon the poor to "Be one of us!" He also asks the poor to acknowledge a wider and deeper poverty that lies beyond the lack of material goods; it is the poverty of values. For man is meant to aspire to *all* goods, to the "whole vastness of the values to which man is called." And the greatest good calls not for anger but for love. *Ubi caritas, ibi Deus.*

On the other side of the discussion taking place within Adam— within his dramatic inner space—is a voice simply dubbed "The Other." The Other seems to represent in some way the mind of the Enlightenment intelligentsia. It calls Adam to a kind of human

30. At one point (*Our God's Brother*, act 2: "In the Vaults of Anger," scene 8: "A Collector for Charity" [*CP*, p. 230]), angered with what he takes to be Adam's sentimentality, the Stranger accuses Adam of leaving the poor doubly depraved: by their own poverty and his handout charity, so that they are robbed of the power to reclaim their dignity.

31. The Stranger harangues Adam: "Ah, charity. A *złoty* here, a *złoty* there, for the right to secure the possession of the millions invested in banks, forests, land, bonds, shares . . . who knows what else. This is what it boils down to in practice. For a *złoty* here, a *złoty* there, marked and accounted for exactly—while at the same time others toil animal-like, ten, twelve, sixteen hours a day for a miserable penny, for less than the right to live, for the hope of a dubious consolation up above, a consolation that changes nothing but has for centuries fettered the mighty, magnificent eruption of human anger—creative human anger." Adam: "Is it possible that you may be right in so much that you have said? . . . But you know, all that is terrible, terrible!" (*Our God's Brother*, act 1 [*CP*, p. 192]).—"A dubious consolation up above": A union orator expresses a similar anger in George Eliot's *Felix Holt* (London: Penguin, 1866) p. 397: "They'll give us plenty of heaven. We may have land there. That's the sort of religion they like—a religion that gives us working men heaven, and nothing else. But we'll offer to change with 'em. We'll give them back some of their heaven, and take it out in something for us and our children in this world."—We find the recognition of injustice also in his papal social encyclicals and in his national addresses (such as those of his Mexican and Canadian visits). But, while he has experienced hunger, cold, and persecution, he— like Adam—has transmuted that suffering not into anger but into the reality of Christian love.

maturity. Adam, however, finds it to be a truncated sort of maturity, because it rests everything upon merely understanding the world as it is without shouldering its burdens.

At this point, Adam finds his own salvation, instead, when he helps a poor man whom he notices leaning wretchedly against a lamp post in the cold dark street. For in that man Adam comes at last to see an image. It is not an easy vision, however, and Adam struggles against the awareness that he must give himself up if he is to identify with this image. He cries out: "How can I cease to be who I am?"[32] Nevertheless, it is through this discovery that Adam is at last able to say, "I am not alone."[33]

The newly discovered image is not, however, the visual image to which his art has given expression, not even the image of *Ecce Homo,* the subject of his latest and best painting. It is not that art does not count. On the contrary, Adam's priest-confessor reassures him that "God regards your art with a father's eye," since it brings people nearer to God through its reflected glory. But Adam has seen a deeper image than art can shape: it is a nonpictorial image, "imperceptible to my eye but that preys upon my soul."[34] Indeed, it is clear that it is the very image of God that is struggling for recognition and realization in his own soul, and in that of the poor man. Calling out to The Other, to the voice of the Enlightenment, Adam shouts with joy over having given up "the tyranny of intelligence," of an intelligence without love, with its "clear image of the world." Instead, he has found a different, deeper, mysterious image. The Other does not or cannot understand him, however, and Adam experiences an exultant liberation: "You don't know! So there is a sphere in my thought that you do not possess."

Is it too much to see here an autobiographical undercurrent in

32. Later (*Our God's Brother,* act 3, "The Brother's Day" [*CP,* p. 249]), a member of Brother Albert's religious community, the cook, says, "We didn't come here to have an easy time."

33. *Our God's Brother,* act 1 (*CP,* p. 185).—Cf. the image of the double tree trunk as the presence of the parent in the child (*Radiation of Fatherhood,* part 2, scene 2 [*CP,* p. 345]); also, how, as Monica enters the stream, the Source embraces her (scene 3 [*CP,* p. 351]).

34. *Our God's Brother,* act 2, scene 2 (*CP,* pp. 204–5).

which the drama plays out, not only the Christian response to both socialist collectivism and to Enlightenment individualism, but also Wojtyła's own renunciation of art as his principal way of life?[35] It is not that others should not pursue art as a vocation, but that Wojtyła himself was called to enter upon another path.

Near the end of the drama Adam, now Brother Albert, speaks to a postulant of a "different sort of art,"[36] the art of serving God through being one with the poor. It is an art prompted by the generosity of God, who has changed the slavery of the fall into the freedom of the Cross. As the play comes to a close, the brothers report an outbreak in the city, an outbreak of that long-repressed, just anger, an act of collective awareness turned against oppressors. Brother Albert recognizes it for what it is and that it is an anger that will last as long as injustice itself. But—and this is one of his last days in a life devoted to the poor—he says quietly, almost to himself: "I know for certain, though, that I have chosen a greater freedom."

∿

The best known of his plays, at least in English, is *The Jeweler's Shop* (published in 1960 under the pseudonym Andrzej Jawień), modestly subtitled: "A Meditation on the Sacrament of Matrimony, Passing on Occasion into a Drama."[37] The structure of the drama is interesting in itself. In addition to the Old Jeweler, the Chorus, and the Christ figure of the Bridegroom, the chief protagonists are seven: three couples and a somewhat mysterious figure, a Chance Interlocutor, who we learn is named Adam and who represents a sort of modern Everyman. He is recognized at the very end as "a common denominator of us all—at the same time a spokesman and a judge."[38] The Old Jeweler is also a shadowy fig-

---

35. It may be that Wojtyła had taken up the study of Polish philology as a preparation for a lifelong career in theater. See Taborski, *CP*, p. 3.

36. *Our God's Brother*, act 3 (*CP*, pp. 256ff.).

37. Taborski (*CP*, pp. 267–75) terms it a poetic drama and suggests that the subtitle downplays the dramatic power of the work. He points also to its innovative form, and mentions similarities with Péguy, Claudel, Pinter, Eliot, and others.

38. *The Jeweler's Shop*, act 3, scene 5 (*CP*, p. 321). Curiously, without naming himself, he names each of the protagonists. And (act 3, scene 4 [*CP*, p. 318]) at

ure; perhaps he speaks for Divine Providence or is the voice of conscience.[39]

The drama divides into three acts, each of which contains, for the most part, alternating monologues, as if spoken out loud but into a surrounding and receptive silence. In the first act we meet Teresa and Andrew during their courtship and impending marriage. It is a short but happy marriage, and the widowed Teresa keeps the presence of Andrew somehow alive within her after he is killed in battle. In the second act we meet Anna and Stefan whose marriage has been broken by a mutual disillusion and anger. In the third act we meet Monica, the daughter of the separated couple, and Christopher, the son of the first couple. The young people are planning to marry. In sum, then, we have a theme: the exploration of married love in and through a brief but happy marriage, at once both sad and joyful; a failed marriage, treated sympathetically and without facile judgment; and a forthcoming marriage, trembling with fear and hope.[40] This threefold structure provides ample dramatic space for an exploration of married love. The present purpose will be best served by emphasis upon two themes among several within the drama.

The first theme explores love as the interplay between mind and reality, between consciousness and existence: these are the noetic and the ontological dimensions of love. Love is at once something intensely conscious and very real. On the one hand, love is the conscious presence of one person in and with another.[41] But it is

---

the wedding he takes the place of Christopher's long-dead father, Andrew, since— as Adam himself observes—he could not die for Andrew. Adam somehow embodies the human nature common to each of us.

39. Suggested by Taborski, *CP*, p. 271.

40. Reflecting upon her own marriage and the forthcoming marriage of the children, Teresa speaks to her absent yet somehow still-present husband: "You have no notion, my husband, how terrible the fear is that borders on hope and penetrates it daily. There is no hope without fear and no fear without hope" (*The Jeweler's Shop*, act 3, scene 1 [*CP*, p. 310]).—Monica, wounded by the rift in her own parents' marriage, asks, "Is human love at all capable of enduring through man's whole experience?" (act 3, scene 2 [*CP*, p. 311]). The tension between existence and love runs throughout the last two acts.

41. At the beginning of their courtship Andrew speaks of "the basis of that strange persistence of Teresa in me, the cause of her presence, the assurance of her

thereby also a union in reality. The Chorus celebrates the union of the first couple: "New People—Teresa and Andrew—two until now but still not one, one from now on though still two."[42] Anna later recalls that Adam had spoken of love as "a synthesis of two people's existence, which converges, as it were, at a certain point and makes them one."[43] But the rift, the brokenness of love in Anna and Stefan, also retains these two dimensions. Anna reflects upon her separation from Stefan, a separation both in consciousness and in reality. Stefan no longer reacts to me, she says to herself: he is no longer present in me; and yet, though I now exist for myself, I am no longer at home in myself. And she ponders the pain inherent in a broken love:

It was as if I had become unaccustomed to the walls of my interior—so full had they been of Stefan that without him they seemed empty. Is it not too terrible a thing to have committed the walls of my interior to a single inhabitant who could disinherit my self and somehow deprive me of my place in it?[44]

Anna is poised on the painful borderline between self-absorption and an openness that is not yet quite closed to love. She searches for the perfect companion, but when the Bridegroom comes along the street—clearly the figure of Christ—she is disconcerted to find in His face the face she hates and fears, the face of Stefan. A process begins in her, as she considers the face of Stefan as it is reflected in the Bridegroom's face and the face of Stefan embodied in her sometime husband. She cannot any longer recover that initial "girlish" infatuation and rapture, since it has "dried up like water which cannot a second time spring from the earth."[45] Nor can she

place in my ego, or what creates around her that strange resonance . . ." (*The Jeweler's Shop,* act 1, scene 1 [*CP,* p. 281]).

42. *The Jeweler's Shop,* act 1, scene 5 (*CP,* p. 290).
43. *The Jeweler's Shop,* act 2, scene 2 (*CP,* p. 300).—When Anna, after the separation, tries to sell her wedding ring, the Old Jeweler will not accept it: "This ring does not weigh anything; the needle does not move from zero, and I cannot make it show even a milligram. Your husband must be alive, in which case neither of your rings, taken separately, will weigh anything—only both together will register. My jeweler's scales have this peculiarity, that they weigh not the metal but man's entire being and fate" (act 2, scene 2 [*CP,* pp. 297–98]).
44. *The Jeweler's Shop,* act 2, scene 1 (*CP,* p. 294).
45. *The Jeweler's Shop,* act 3, scene 5 (*CP,* p. 319).—The image occurs earlier,

erase the "disproportion" between the faces, which is in fact a disproportion between existence and love.[46] Though the faces are somehow the same, she cannot bring herself to identify them. Still, some healing has begun: with a sense of her own share of responsibility for the breakup, she arrives at something a little short of forgiveness; and finally, at the sense that she and Stefan have become "less burdensome" in each other's presence. Through her suffering Anna has learned—perhaps better than Stefan—something deeper about the meaning of love. In intimate conversation with Adam—Adam, after all, is somehow in solidarity with her own humanity and with all humanity—she has come to reject her immature notion that love is "a matter of the senses and of a climate which unites and makes two people walk in the sphere of their feeling."[47] And yet, while love is not simply emotion, neither is it thought or imagination cut off from the whole of life. When Anna asks: "With what is thought to remain, then?" Adam replies: "With truth."[48] Thought plays a role in love, but in the end we cannot answer why we love; love is—in dry philosophical terms—the first principle, which gives meaning to everything else. Christopher speaks of his love for Monica:

Why does one love at all? What do I love you for, Monica? Don't ask me to answer. I couldn't say. Love outdistances its object or approaches it so

---

as Adam speaks to Anna on behalf of the Bridegroom (Christ): "Beloved, you do not know how deeply you are mine, how much you belong to my love and my suffering—because to love means to give life through death; to love means to let gush a spring of the water of life into the depths of the soul, which burns or smolders and cannot burn out. Ah, the flame and the spring. You don't feel the spring, but are consumed by the flame. Is that not so?" (act 2, scene 3 [*CP*, pp. 305–6]).

46. Adam observes: "Sometimes human existence seems too short for love. At other times, however, it is the other way around: human love is too short in relation to existence—or rather too trivial" (*The Jeweler's Shop*, act 3, scene 5 [*CP*, p. 321]).—Cf. also, act 1, scene 3 (*CP*, p. 288): "A disproportion between the wish for happiness and a man's potential is unavoidable." But, then, too, the Chorus reminds us that, if the disproportion is to be remedied, "Man will not suffice" (act 1, scene 5 [*CP*, p. 292]).

47. *The Jeweler's Shop*, act 2, scene 2 (*CP*, p. 300).—Earlier Andrew had said: "I simply resisted sensation and the appeal of the senses, for I knew that otherwise I would never really leave my ego and reach the other person—but that meant an effort [of the will] . . . I wanted to regard love as passion, as an emotion to surpass all—I believed in the absolute of emotion" (act 1, scene 1 [*CP*, pp. 280–81]).

48. *The Jeweler's Shop*, act 2, scene 2 (*CP*, p. 300).

closely that it is almost lost from view. Man must then think differently, must leave cold deliberations—and in that "hot thinking" one question is important: Is it creative?[49]

If the first theme plays out the relation in love between consciousness and reality, the second probes the depths of love. For love has both surface and depth. Christopher urges Monica to look more deeply into her parents in order to see the love with which they have nourished her: "People have their depths, not only the masks on their faces."[50] Adam, too, finds a paradox in love:

There is no other matter embedded more strongly in the surface of human life, and there is no matter more unknown and more mysterious. The divergence between what lies on the surface of the mystery of love constitutes precisely the source of the drama. It is one of the greatest dramas of human existence. The surface of love has its current—swift, flickering, changeable. A kaleidoscope of waves and situations full of attraction. This current is sometimes so stunning that it carries people away—women and men. They get carried away by the thought that they have absorbed the whole secret of love, but in fact they have not yet even touched it. They are happy for a while, thinking they have reached the limits of existence and wrested all its secrets from it, so that nothing remains. That's how it is [in their view]: on the other side of that rapture nothing remains, there is nothing left behind it.

Adam pauses, and with new vehemence, protests: "But there can't be nothing; there can't! Listen to me, there can't. Man is a continuum, a totality and a continuity—so it cannot be that nothing remains."[51]

The conversation turns then upon the relation between the temporal surface of love and its eternal depth. Love is less a matter of time than of eternity.[52] It is not an adventure of the passing moment, since it is shot through with that vertical axis that "cuts

49. *The Jeweler's Shop,* act 3, scene 2 (*CP,* p. 313).
50. *The Jeweler's Shop,* act 3, scene 3 (*CP,* pp. 316–17): "All that [caring] cannot pass without leaving a trace."
51. *The Jeweler's Shop,* act 3, scene 3 (*CP,* pp. 301–2).
52. In *The Jeweler's Shop,* act 1, scene 1 (*CP,* p. 279), Teresa notices a certain quality of eternity about love: she recalls the moment when Andrew proposed to her, and observes: "At such moments one does not check the hour, such moments grow in one above time."

across every marriage."[53] Adam's reflection upon the source of love highlights the contrast between surface and depth, adventure and drama, the empty and the full, the part and the whole, the momentary now and the eternal forever. The contrast invites the connection of human love with its source. Adam softly says to Anna: "Ah, Anna, how am I to prove to you that on the other side of all those loves that fill our lives there is Love!"[54] And in his last speech, meditating upon the rift between Anna and Stefan, Adam observes: "The thing is that love carries people away like an absolute, although it [human love] lacks absolute dimensions. But acting under an illusion, they do not try to connect that love with the Love that has such a dimension."[55]

It is not only a matter of the connection between human love and Absolute Love. Within the sphere of human love itself, the love of the parents forms a base in the children and has a hand in shaping their love for one another. Meditating upon the relation between parents and children, Teresa notices "how heavily we all weigh upon their fate. Take Monica's heritage: the rift of that love is so deeply embedded in her that her own love stems from a rift too."[56] It is inevitable, then, that in order to forge their own new love, children must cross the "threshold" of their parents' love "to reach their new homes." It may seem to parents that their children grow inaccessible, like "impermeable soil"; but in truth, she con-

53. *The Jeweler's Shop*, act 3, scene 3 (CP, p. 316).—Adam to Anna: "Love is not an adventure. It has the flavor of the whole man. It has his weight and the weight of his whole fate. It cannot be a single moment. Man's eternity passes through it. That is why it is to be found in the dimensions of God, because only He is eternity. Man looking out into time, to forget, to forget. To be for a moment only—only now—and cut himself off from eternity. To take in everything at one moment and lose everything immediately after. Ah, the curse of that next moment and all the moments that follow, moments through which he will look for the way back to the moment that has passed, to have it once more, and through it—everything" (act 2, scene 3 [CP, p. 303]).—Cf. the despair over the search for the "beautiful moment" in Sartre's *Nausea*.

54. *The Jeweler's Shop*, act 2, scene 3 (CP, p. 305).

55. *The Jeweler's Shop*, act 3, scene 5 (CP, p. 320). He continues: "They do not even feel the need, blinded as they are not so much by the force of their emotion as by lack of humility. They lack humility toward what love must be in its true essence. The more aware they are of it, the smaller the danger. Otherwise the danger is great: love will not stand the pressure of reality."

56. *The Jeweler's Shop*, act 3, scene 3 (CP, p. 314).

fides, "they have already absorbed us. And though outwardly they shut themselves off, inwardly we remain in them"—for good and/ or ill.

Children are marked by the quality of their parents' love for one another. On the one hand, Christopher has been given an "idea of Father"[57] through his mother's continuing love for her dead husband, but he himself has no actual memory of his father. He therefore lacks ready models of manhood, and he does not know "what a man ought to be." Nevertheless, he is called to fatherhood by his love for Monica. Monica, on the other hand, is at first afraid *of* Christopher and afraid *for* herself; but as she falls more deeply in love with him, she reverses the order, and now becomes afraid *of* her inability to love adequately, and becomes afraid *for* Christopher. She warns him: "You are taking a difficult girl, sensitive to a fault, who easily withdraws into herself and only with effort breaks the circle constantly created by her ego."[58] Christopher can only reply that "love is a constant challenge, thrown to us by God," and in going forward together they must take upon themselves the risk of separation through death (as with Andrew, Christopher's father) or even through estrangement (as with Monica's parents). In his last speech Adam agrees that

every person has at his disposal an existence and a love. The problem is how to build a sensible structure from it. But this structure must never be inward looking. It must be open in such a way that, on the one hand, it embraces other people, while, on the other, it always reflects the absolute Existence and Love; it must always, *in some way,* reflect them. That is the ultimate sense of your lives.[59]

57. *The Jeweler's Shop,* act 3, scene 2 (*CP,* p. 311). The reference is to God the Father.—See also *Radiation,* part 1, scene 2 (*CP,* p. 336), where a still defiant Adam worries, "Would people merely associate me always with the idea of the Father?"

58. *The Jeweler's Shop,* act 3, scene 2 (*CP,* pp. 311–13).—Teresa had already remarked (act 3, scene 1 [*CP,* p. 309]): "She was a shy and delicate child—made on me the impression of a being enclosed in herself—whose true value gravitates inward so much that it simply ceases to reach other people."—But Monica's love for Christopher begins to take her out of herself somewhat. Unlike Teresa and Andrew, however, the children take no notice of the Old Jeweler. Monica explains: "We were taken up with each other. . . . All the beauty remained in our own feeling. . . . I was absorbed by my love—and by nothing else it seems" (act 3, scene 3 [*CP,* p. 315]).

59. *The Jeweler's Shop,* act 3, scene 5 (*CP,* p. 321).

With that he names each of the six characters personally by name: Teresa! Andrew! Anna! Stefan! and yours: Monica! Christopher!

Meanwhile, Anna and Stefan seem to have made some progress. Through the pain of their separation, each has come to a deeper realization of the demands of love. Anna regrets that she and Stefan have destroyed so much of the basis of trust within Monica. On the other hand, Adam tells us that Anna's encounter with the Bridegroom has awakened in her a new sense of love, a sort of "complementary love," unlike ordinary love. The last speech is left to Stefan, who confesses that he does not understand what it means "to reflect . . . absolute existence and love," but he does realize that he and Anna have in fact reflected love very badly and that their daughter Monica has paid a terrible price for their lack of love. With sudden insight, he turns to Anna and says plaintively: "What a pity that for so many years we have not felt ourselves to be a couple of children. Anna, Anna, how much we have lost because of that!"[60]

∾

The last drama is entitled: *Radiation of Fatherhood. A Mystery.*[61] It undoubtedly represents the maturation of Wojtyła's efforts at inner drama. The mystery of humanity evokes the emblem of his own theater of the word and augurs his later anthropology. In a scene between father and child (Adam and Monica) that mystery is embodied in a double image of dense vibrancy. The child is at the edge of a forest in which paths wander, crisscrossing one another, leading to hidden places and mysterious encounters. The father presents himself to his child as carrying about within himself an all-but-impenetrable thicket. Monica asks him: "When will

60. *The Jeweler's Shop*, act 3, scene 5 (*CP*, pp. 319–22).—The theme "You must become as little children . . ." has already emerged in *Our God's Brother* (act 2, scene 2 [*CP*, pl 205]).

61. In 1964 *Znak* published a short piece of poetic prose by A. J. entitled: *Reflections on Fatherhood*. The full drama (written somewhat earlier) under its present title was published in the same journal in Nov. 1979; the drama was performed in Warsaw in June 1983 (See Taborski, *CP*, pp. 323, 327).—Many passages are common, even verbatim, to the prose *Reflections* and the dramatic *Radiation*, and in what follows I will treat them as substantially the same in theme and intent, while noting the source in these notes.

be spoken what is contained in you and me, what lies in the depth of consciousness and must wait for words? Being together, shall we find one day the moments for such words that bring to the surface what really is deep down?"[62] The double image of forest and thicket gives way in the next scene to that of a stream whose current can carry father and child to the inexhaustible Source from which the Fatherhood of love radiates.[63] Józef Tischner remarks that *Radiation of Fatherhood* "attempts to lead us to the origins of all human drama . . . the great metaphysics of a sad physics of our world," "the beautiful but also cruel physics of this world."[64]

It is not misleading, it seems to me, to characterize the three parts of the drama as follows: In the first we see humanity embodied in Adam as he struggles with his fallen condition. In the second we glimpse the revelation of the trinitarian love within God as it begins to shed its light within the conversation of father and daughter (Adam and Monica), and as it introduces a new energy into their relationship. In the third part we participate with the Mother in humanity's struggle with the hope that has been generated by the promise of fulfillment.

We begin with Adam—the common denominator of humanity—who finds himself exiled from himself, from his deeper personality, and "yet condemned to probe it."[65] The stage is crowded with people, each absorbed in themselves, passing each other by without notice. Adam senses in each person, as well as in himself, the substance of an unrealized humanity; and yet he fears the loss of his own selfhood in the world about him. He fears the loss of self in the transience of the historical process and the anonymity of mass and number that so dominate our modern world. Adam realizes that he must probe the self not from without but from within. And later he insists that "it is not enough to look from the

62. *Radiation of Fatherhood*, part 2. "The Experience of a Child," scene 2. "The Child's Sanctuary" (*CP*, p. 346).

63. *Radiation of Fatherhood*, part 2, scene 4 (*CP*, pp. 352ff.).

64. From his program notes to the Warsaw production, "Radiation of Creative Interaction," quoted by Taborski, *CP*, pp. 326, 331.

65. *Radiation of Fatherhood*, part 1, scene 1 (*CP*, p. 335). Also in *Reflections on Fatherhood* (*CP*, p. 365).

outside," to approach oneself and others as so many objects; but that one must enter within.[66] It comes to this: Adam complains that God might have left him like the other animals, to multiply and flourish on the earth, instead of inflicting upon him something of God's own spiritual personality.[67] But there it is, and we must now take humanity from the inside, from its experiences and not just from its external behavior. Later still, his daughter Monica recalls her father's belated complaint that "too many of the bonds between us are external; there are too few inner bonds."[68] Authentic fatherhood entails an intimate relationship with one's child.

Adam describes himself as Everyman, as the common denominator for that loneliness which humanity has chosen.[69] Indeed, this loneliness is a specific condition, a condition of the species, the elective fate of humankind. We have here, it seems to me, nothing less than a dramatic representation of the fallen situation of man.[70] A certain lethargy sustains this loneliness; Adam finds it easier to feel lonely than to contemplate his actual situation, for that requires him to confront his mortality.[71] He tries to evade his true origin and the call to fatherhood.[72] Excusing himself before God, he pleads: Did I not call from the start, "Leave me my loneliness?"[73] Poised on the border between fatherhood and loneliness,

66. *Radiation of Fatherhood*, part 2, scene 3 (*CP*, p. 347).

67. *Radiation of Fatherhood*, part 1, scene 2 (*CP*, p. 337): "Did You have to touch my thought with Your knowledge that means giving birth? Did You have to touch my will with the love that is fulfillment?"

68. *Radiation of Fatherhood*, part 2, scene 5 (*CP*, p. 356).

69. *Reflections on Fatherhood* (*CP*, pp. 365–66): "Although I am like the man who can be placed apart and then made a common denominator for all men, I still remain lonely." Such objective universality leaves Adam "still a common denominator for everyone, which can be substituted for anyone or a common word that can be put outside the brackets."—In *Radiation of Fatherhood*, part 1, scene 4 (*CP*, p. 339), Adam, speaking to the Father: "When Your Son came, I remained the common denominator of man's inner loneliness."

70. *Radiation of Fatherhood*, part 1, scene 2 (*CP*, p. 336); *Reflections on Fatherhood* (*CP*, p. 365).

71. *Radiation of Fatherhood*, part I: "Adam," scene 2: "The Analysis of Loneliness" (*CP*, p. 336): "It is easier for me to feel lonely than to think about death. . . . I find it easier to feel lonely than guilty of sin."

72. *Radiation of Fatherhood*, part 1, scene 2 (*CP*, p. 338). Adam admits to "continually evading Your Fatherhood and gravitating toward my loneliness."

73. *Radiation of Fatherhood*, part 1, scene 2 (*CP*, p. 337).

Adam has sought to be more like God; but by this likeness he means: insofar as God is "independent of everything."[74] The conflict is then, if I have understood it correctly, not between an Adam-with-God and an Adam-wholly-without-God, for no creature can exist in the total absence of God. Ultimately Adam's quarrel with God is over two images of God that may define Adam: the image of self-subsistence and the image of relatedness. Adam insists upon choosing the version of self-subsistence. He chooses his own version of what it is to be in the image of God, rather than accepting the actual image that God has conferred upon Adam. Adam chooses the ideal of self-sufficiency and autonomy, rather than the community of shared love realized in the trinitarian Godhead.[75] Later, Adam concedes that his eyes were too fixed upon himself.[76] He wants to have everything through himself and not through God, even though he knows that such absolute independence is not possible.[77]

At one point Adam tenders God a bargain: Why not split man up into a worldly, outward Adam and an inward, lonely Adam? Into public object and private subject? Into organism and psyche? That, he tells God, would leave the outward Adam to nourish the offspring God seems to desire, while the inward Adam could nurse his own loneliness. And that, Adam concludes, would cleave man in two without touching his inner loneliness.[78] It seems to me that

74. *Radiation of Fatherhood*, part 1, scene 2 (*CP*, p. 336); also *Reflections on Fatherhood* (*CP*, p. 365).—In *Radiation*, part 1, scene 2 (*CP*, p. 336): Adam "stopped once on the frontier between fatherhood and loneliness. . . . What if he became lonely of his own free will?—In the *Original Unity of Man and Woman* (1979–80) John Paul II discusses the "original solitude" of Adam at length (see chap. 4, below); here in the drama Adam hankers after that solitude but on his own terms.

75. Józef Tischner remarks: "The God of Christianity is not an Absolute Solitude but an Absolute Interaction" of divine Persons (cited in *CP*, p. 327).

76. *Radiation of Fatherhood*, part 1, scene 4: "Between Meeting and Fulfillment" (*CP*, p. 339).

77. *Radiation of Fatherhood*, part 1, scene 2 (*CP*, p. 337). Indeed, Adam pronounces his wish "nonsense," but observes wryly that that has not stopped people from pursuing it.

78. *Radiation of Fatherhood*, part 1, scene 2 (*CP*, p. 337) and scene 4 (*CP*, p. 340).—Cf. (above) Max's "exchangeable" outer man and his inner "nonexchangeable" man in *Our God's Brother*, act 1 (*CP*, pp. 164ff.).

this separation of public externality and private inwardness is pretty much the conventional wisdom put forth by many in our modern world.

Adam finds a strange ambiguity in the word "mine." In its negative sense it means "not yours"; and in the final analysis that means "not God's." The very word itself is relational, even correlative. When it is applied, not simply in an external fashion to the possession of property, but inwardly to the relation between persons, the very word cancels loneliness, because it cannot exclude from its meaning a reference to what is not mine, to what is "yours." And so, against his will, Adam is forced to realize that the very word leads him back towards God. At this point he defiantly decides to abandon the term itself; only to find that the private self is thereby imperilled.[79] For Adam's loneliness is disclosed as a nullity that loses the very sense of self, either by being driven back into an absolute isolation beyond what is mine or yours, or by being poured out into a common denominator that is neither exclusively mine or yours.

If Adam is lonely by choice, still—as the common denominator of humankind—his loneliness is contagious. Indeed, the emptiness of that common denominator is the basis for the contagion of loneliness. Yet such loneliness is not what God intended when he created human nature. Rather, Adam grafts his loneliness upon others.[80] Later, the figure of the Mother will observe that Adam's children "walk naked from within." Outwardly they are clothed

79. *Radiation of Fatherhood*, part 1, scene 2 (*CP*, p. 337): "I am afraid of the word 'mine,' though at the same time I cherish its meaning. . . . An analysis of the word 'mine' always leads me to You. And I would rather give up using it than find its ultimate sense in You" (*Reflections on Fatherhood* [*CP*, p. 366]).—Cf. Psalm 49. It is interesting that the dialectic anticipates, even while it proposes an answer to, the current critique by Derrida and other Deconstructionists, who attack the very notions of the self, authorship, and authority.

80. *Radiation of Fatherhood*, part 1, scene 2 (*CP*, p. 336–37); Adam speaks: "When I give birth, I do it to become lonely among those born, because I pass on to them the germ of loneliness. In the midst of a multitude, are they not more and more lonely?" The use of the word "graft" indicates that the loneliness is an imposition upon human nature and not of its essence: human nature is wounded but not destroyed (also *Reflections on Fatherhood* [*CP*, p. 365]).—Yet such a contagion forms "the strangest community—the community of loneliness" (*Radiation of Fatherhood*, part 3 [*CP*, p. 360]).

with the products of their own work and with those of other creatures, but "on the inside they are naked."[81]

Because of Adam's self-willed closure—his resistance to God's
communication to him and within him—Adam finds the invitation to participate in God's own fatherhood to be not a gift but a
burden, an intrusion upon his loneliness.[82] Adam finds it unrea-
sonable of God to want to let his divine Fatherhood enter into
Adam's selfhood, for then Adam would reflect the radiation of
divine Fatherhood as a prism refracts light. In a word: Adam rejects the burden of carrying the image of God within him and of
communicating it to others.[83] He complains that it is too great a
risk to be a true father to a child. It is the risk inherent in the call
to love, that "constant challenge" of which Christopher has spoken
in *The Jeweler's Shop*.[84]

Still, Adam struggles with the challenge. He comes to recognize
that loneliness is not ultimate in him: "not at the bottom of my
being at all." This is because there is a deeper fissure in his being
than any subsequent closure, an open sesame into which God
makes his way. This fissure is not the rift explored in *The Jeweler's
Shop*; for that rift is not original but comes later and not without
human choice. Surely, the fissure is the "place" for the influx of
the creative existence that sustains Adam at the cutting edge of his
being.[85] It is an absolute opening, an opening for the Father's love,

81. *Radiation of Fatherhood*, part 3, scene 1 (*CP*, p. 361).
82. *Radiation of Fatherhood*, part 1, scene 2 (*CP*, p. 336): "I could not bear
fatherhood; I could not be equal to it. I felt totally helpless—and what had been
a gift became a burden to me."
83. *Radiation of Fatherhood*, part 1, scene 2 (*CP*, p. 337). In this context the
image relation is one of "mine" and "Yours."
84. *The Jeweler's Shop*, act 3, scene 2 (*CP*, p. 312), "thrown to us by God,
thrown, I think, so that we should challenge fate." Fate here is the destiny inherent
in our fallen nature, the rule of sin.
85. *Radiation of Fatherhood*, part 1, scene 3 (*CP*, p. 338); Adam speaks:
". . . You are never against me. You enter into what I call loneliness, and You overcome my resistance. Can one say that You force Your way in or only that You enter
through a door that is open anyway? You did not make me closed; You did not
quite close me. Loneliness is not at the bottom of my being at all; it grows at a
certain point. The fissure through which You enter is far deeper. You enter—and
slowly begin to shape me. You shape and develop me in spite of what I imagine
about my ego and other people, yet You do it in harmony with what I am."

that Absolute Love already present in the earlier dramas. Thus, for example, it is the face of her separated husband as it is reflected in the face of the Bridegroom that works upon Anna and gradually makes Stefan's presence "less burdensome" to her.

Adam understands that the opposition founded in conflict is meant to give way to a harmony that endorses his own integrity. But the challenge of love continues, and the risk continues with it. Perhaps we should interpret Adam's struggle as a struggle with that original solitude mentioned in Genesis, prior to the creation of woman, and which we will explore in the fourth chapter. Or rather, the struggle is with what Adam might have suffered had God left him in that solitude. At any rate, Adam seems here to recount his own fall. The very success of creation tempts Adam toward a drift: "Gradually I cease to feel that You express Yourself in me, and I begin to think that I express myself in myself."[86] But then a sense of nonfulfillment arises within Adam, caused—not simply by desire—but by a certain withdrawal from that original Love. A void wells up within him on the borderline of that orig-inal-solitude-now-become-loneliness.[87] The void mingles Adam's as-yet-untransformed loneliness with the suffering inseparable from the call to love, a call that is daunting to Adam in his loneliness. For the suffering arises only through the muted presence of a Love whose absence is nevertheless felt and somehow understood.[88]

It is here that a pivotal scene takes up the theme of "The Thresh-old Crossed by Woman." The Woman is undoubtedly Eve, but also Everywoman and each woman; is she also Mary? and the Church? At any rate, she enters Adam's loneliness perhaps at several levels, so that Adam is able to move from the pole of loneliness toward the pole of love.[89] The Woman conceives a child and gives to Adam

---

86. *Radiation of Fatherhood*, part 1, scene 3 (*CP*, p. 338).

87. *Radiation of Fatherhood*, part 1, scene 2 (*CP*, p. 338); Adam is poised "between the upper borderline of man filled with humanity and the lower one of humanity destroyed in man."

88. *Radiation of Fatherhood*, part 2, scene 4 (*CP*, p. 353). Adam to Monica: "Every feeling, my child, must be permeated by light. . . . One must transfix feelings with thought."

89. *Radiation of Fatherhood*, part 3, scene 1 (*CP*, p. 360). It seems to me that,

a new sense of "mine," that very sense which he had resisted. He had resisted because, while his own fatherhood would break down his loneliness, it would also lead him to the Father whose very being is Fatherhood. It is through the child, then, that Adam becomes a father. He says, half complaining: "You want me to love. You aim at me through a child, through a tiny daughter or son—and my resistance weakens."[90]

But Adam arrives at a deeper truth, a truth that arises out of his not-entirely-willing recognition of the image of God that is present in him through the fissure. He realizes that the radiation of the Father's love consists in giving birth, even as from all eternity the Father is Father through begetting His Son: "We return to the father through the child."[91] What is more, Adam comes to realize that—according to the logic of existence embedded in everything—he can accept the radiation of Love from the Father in and through the Son, only by therewith becoming himself a son, and once again a child: "To absorb the radiation of fatherhood means not only to become a father but, much more, to become a child."[92] Adam says: "After a long time I came to understand that

---

at the first entrance (*Radiation*, part 1, scene 3, *CP*, p. 339), the Woman is Eve and Everywoman, but that here she is the Woman of Faith, hence Mary and the Church, and whoever—woman and men—live out of that faith.

90. *Radiation of Fatherhood*, part 1, scene 3 (*CP*, p. 338). The same holds for the Mother (*CP*, p. 339). And at part 3, scene 1 (*CP*, p. 362), speaking to the newborn child, the Woman says: "This is also the moment of my birth, the moment in which I become a Mother." Although Adam's resistance is weakened, he still warns Monica: "Is it not true that in the word 'father' there is also fear? I will never be only stillness but also storm. Nor will I be sweetness only; I will add bitterness. And though I try to be transparent, I will also be a puzzle" (part 2, scene 5 [*CP*, p. 356]). Earlier the Chorus asks: "Where has the exiled father gone to? Where has the punishing father come from?" (part 1, scene 4 [*CP*, p. 340]). It is possible that these words, once transformed by that Absolute Love Who is Mercy, might also adumbrate the divine Father.

91. *Radiation of Fatherhood*, part 1, scene 5 (*CP*, p. 341).

92. *Reflections on Fatherhood* (*CP*, p. 368). Cf. Stefan to Anna, *The Jeweler's Shop*, act 3, scene 5 (*CP*, pp. 319–22). The insistence upon becoming once again a child undoubtedly follows from Jesus' injunction: "Unless you become as little children. . . ." In sharp contrast to Wojtyła's emphasis, Descartes all but complains that we would have been better off if from the start we had been born with fully adult human reasons (*Discourse* I-II), and Kant in his essay *What is Enlightenment?* holds forth the escape from dependency (tutelage) as the beginning of mature humanity.

you do not want me to become a father unless I become a child."[93] The image within Adam is the image of "my" Father and "yours," Who has begotten the Word, and of his Spirit who proceeds from their Love. Father, child and love: that is what is essential, what remains.[94]

Throughout the drama the Mother—especially in the third and last part—remains a mysterious figure; perhaps the author intended it so. If on her first entrance she may be mostly Eve, or Everywoman and each woman, in the last part she seems also to stand for the Church, and within the Church for Mary. She speaks of herself as the least obtrusive of the servants of history, bringing to mind the *Magnificat*.

Already in part two, in the child's sanctuary, we find that the stream, which is at once the edge of earth and of human thought, is not an ordinary stream. Just after being rescued from a viper on the trail, Monica puts her feet in the cool, refreshing water of the forest stream: it is "the water that has given birth to man anew"— surely a reference to baptism.[95]

Moreover, the Mother is not herself the light, since that Light radiates from the Father; but she is the shade that protects, and she herself glows with an inner radiance which she communicates to the children of Adam.[96] Each time, she counsels: "Adam, accept the radiation of fatherhood; Adam, become a child." But each

---

93. *Radiation of Fatherhood*, part 1, scene 4 (*CP*, p. 339). What is more, in the constant giving of birth, "the father revives [as father] in the soil of the child's soul" (*CP*, p. 340).

94. *Radiation of Fatherhood*, part 3, scene 2 (*CP*, p. 364). Also *Reflections on Fatherhood* (*CP*, p. 368): "And everything else will then turn out to be unimportant and inessential, except for this: father, child, and love."—It seems that the secret formula of which Adam speaks at *Radiation* part 2, scene 5 (*CP*, p. 358) is the Trinity; cf. n. 75.

95. *Radiation of Fatherhood*, part 2, scene 3 (*CP*, p. 350).

96. *Radiation of Fatherhood*, part 3, scene 1, "Concern for Inner Radiance" (*CP*, pp. 360–61). The Mother: "I gather the people whom Adam has dispersed. There is in me a love stronger than loneliness. That love is not of me. . . . I love Adam and constantly restore to him the fatherhood he renounces. I discreetly turn his loneliness into my motherhood. . . . And I am not the light of those I enlighten but rather a shade in which they rest. . . . I do not know how it happens that I fill these people with radiance from within. Or rather I do know, but my knowledge is faith."

time Adam is silent; he does not hear or want to hear. She expresses her fatigue more than once toward the close of the drama, and at one point she whispers: "Oh, Adam, how tired I am of you. Truly, fatigue is the measure of our love." But she answers the call of the Bridegroom, and calls in turn to Adam's children to "take into yourself the light that will guide you through Adam's loneliness and lead you to the Father."[97]

Now, Adam knows that the love she communicates to all humankind liberates men and women from loneliness. Indeed, it liberates from an unattached freedom, and gives rise to a new, more certain freedom.[98] For the fullness of God is the denial of the emptiness of loneliness.[99] But Adam also realizes that the same light leads straight through the Invisible Child who rests in the Mother's arms, and that it must pass through the suffering and death of that Child, as well as through the death of all human fatherhood and human childhood. And with that Adam is brought back to the thought he has tried to evade throughout the drama: the realization of his mortality.

A troubled Adam remains poised in a quandary between two choices: the loneliness of his own self-isolation, or the adopted fatherhood-childhood that must pass through suffering and death. Adam has known all these things: he has known that the Father is the Source who shows the way, and that the Father could retreat without loss within the Godhead to the absolute Love between Father and Child, leaving the whole world to its self-destruction. The chorus echoes Adam's desperate sigh: "Could we not have learned this long ago? Has this not always been embedded in every-

97. *Radiation of Fatherhood*, part 3, scene 1 (*CP*, p. 362). It is here that she adds, "This is also the moment of my birth, the moment in which I become a Mother."

98. *Radiation of Fatherhood*, part 2, scenes 4–5 (*CP*, pp. 355–56): "Love denies freedom of will to him who loves—love liberates him from the freedom that would be terrible to have for its own sake. . . . What remains is to await a new maturity, a new unity of will, a common rhythm . . . when we love, a common current runs through our wills. From it a certainty grows, and freedom is born again from certainty. And this is what love means. And then without fear I think 'mine'."

99. *Reflections on Fatherhood* (*CP*, p. 368).

thing that is?"[100] But the drama closes with the Mother's clarion voice: "You are wrong, Adam! You are all wrong! In me will survive the heritage of all men, implanted in the Bridegroom's death."

In *Reflections on Fatherhood*, Adam says: "All this I know. But is it enough? Knowing, I can continue to substitute for everything the same old common denominator of my loneliness—my inner loneliness, chosen so that I can remain myself alone and nobody else."[101] And again, in his conversation with Monica, Adam asks, "When we descend from word to will, what will the word mean?"[102]

We are left at the close of the drama, then, with an indecisive Adam, a sort of universal Hamlet; he needs something more than the knowledge he has: he needs to *act*.[103] It is, then, to Karol Wojtyła's exploration of the requisites for human action that we next turn.

---

100. *Radiation of Fatherhood*, part 3, scene 2, "Radiation and Dying" (*CP*, p. 368). *Reflections on Fatherhood* (*CP*, p. 368) closes on this note.

101. *Reflections on Fatherhood* (*CP*, p. 368). Is this not the same "knowledge without love" against which (in *Our God's Brother*) the future Brother Albert protests to the Other, i.e., to the voice of the Enlightenment? Or again, in *Jeremiah*, when Father Peter cries out that "words are not enough!"

102. *Radiation of Fatherhood*, part 2, scene 5 (*CP*, p. 357). It is not too much to see here a dramatic form of Wojtyła's philosophical concern with ethical action and its foundations, a concern to which we turn in the following chapters.

103. In *Rhapsodies of the Millenium* (*CP*, pp. 385–86) Wojtyła illustrates the drama of moral values by reference to the legend of Mieczysław in which a newly Christian people's collective action topples the statue of the "god" Światowid. At once horrified yet determined, proud yet humble, they tremble before the unseen consequences of the act. This, he observes, is "a drama of the highest order, a drama in the sphere of values." And in *Forefathers' Eve* (*CP*, p. 389) he speaks of a "theater of specific action," of "multidimensional action," and of the moral task of such drama.

CHAPTER II

At the Lublin Workshop
Retrieving the Tradition

In his dramas of the inner word we have witnessed Karol Wojtyła's intense interest in the nature of human action. Through the means of dramatic action he has explored the ambiguities of the human condition and the possibilities of acting for good and/ or evil. The dramatist Wojtyła carries this exploration over into the thought of the philosopher Wojtyła. Make no mistake about it, within the many facets of his mind and personality philosophy holds a treasured place. A philosopher from Latin America visited me not so long ago and told me that, after concluding the business of his interview with the pope, the latter glanced at the time and said: "Good! We have some time. I am a philosopher, you know; so let's talk philosophy." Wojtyła has acquired a thoroughly modern knowledge of philosophy and has assimilated one of its modern approaches—phenomenology—to his own thinking.[1] His doctoral dissertation engaged a leading philosopher of this bent (Max Scheler), and Wojtyła himself has continued a spate of philosophical (as well as other) publications throughout his busy ecclesiastical career.

Wojtyła's special interest in philosophy is in ethics, but that interest is worked out in the larger context of the nature, condition, and destiny of the human person. This has come to be called philosophical anthropology. Up until very recently in North

---

1. In his introduction to *Primat des Geistes. Philosophische Schriften* (ed. Juliusz Stroynowski, foreword by Andrzej Półtawski [Stuttgart-Degerloch: Seewald Verlag, 1980], p. 19; hereafter *PG*), Manfred S. Frings, an authority on phenomenology and on the philosophy of Max Scheler, remarks, "Karol Wojtyła is extraordinarily well versed in contemporary philosophy."—Translations from the German are mine throughout.

America the term "anthropology" has been more or less restricted to the discipline or set of disciplines within the special sciences with which our university departments acquaint us: physical anthropology draws upon paleontology, physiology, and related disciplines, and cultural anthropology draws upon archaeology, sociology, psychology, linguistics, and related disciplines. This is still the common usage of the term in North America. One of the European senses of the term, however—which is Wojtyła's sense as well—takes into account these positive scientific studies, but the sense of the term is above all philosophical, and appears also within theology as a branch of that study. In the fourth chapter, we will consider something of John Paul II's theological anthropology,[2] but Wojtyła's elaboration of a philosophical understanding of the human person will occupy us for this and the following chapter.

His philosophical anthropology finds expression in numerous publications which appeared in book form or in learned journals and semi-popular periodicals. I will trace the formation of his anthropology, however, as it comes to expression principally in two major works. They are the *Lublin Lectures,* which he gave from 1954 to 1957 as Professor of Ethics at the Catholic University of Lublin, and *Person and Act,* which appeared in Polish in 1969 and later in English under the title, *The Acting Person.*[3]

The question that stimulates Karol Wojtyła throughout these two works on the foundations of ethics is nothing less than the hoary question: Why be moral? Why should I do what I should, rather than what I would? Why ought I to do what is right? There are many quick answers to that question, of course. Among them

2. See the Appendix: John Grondelski, "Sources for the Study of Karol Wojtyła's Thought," especially items 25, 81, and 90; hereafter, Grondelski with the numbered item, as in [Grondelski items 25, 81, 90].

3. I will cite from the *Lublin Lectures* in the German translation: *Lubliner Vorlesungen,* ed. Juliusz Stroynowski, foreword by Tadeusz Styczeń (Stuttgart-Degerloch: Seewald Verlag, 1981); hereafter cited within parentheses in the text as *LV* with page number. Here too the translations from the German are mine.— As for *Osoba i czyn* (Cracow: Polskie Towarzystwo Teologiczne, 1969) (Eng. trans.: *The Acting Person*), see the controverted details of the English edition below, chap. 3, nn. 2ff.; hereafter cited within parentheses in the text as *AP* with page number [Grondelski, item 48].

are: "Because I'll get caught if I don't"; this arises from the fear of punishment and is one of the external bonds of which the plays speak. Or again: "Because I was brought up that way"; this arises out of fidelity to custom. Or yet again: "Because I have a sense that it is good to do what is good"; and this is the insight that comes with sound character. In a relatively stable and traditional society we might get by with such answers, but today we do not live in a traditional society.

To live in a traditional society is to live in more or less immediate touch with the relevant past. Instead, today we have continually to attempt to reinvent that past, that is to say: recover it. I once had a devout traditional Moslem as a doctoral candidate. He was immensely learned in his own tradition, but I had great difficulty in getting him to use the latest critical editions of Arabic philosophers (edited mainly by Francophone scholars). He did not see why he should consult such products of Western learning, since he had received the only "correct" tradition from his master, who had received it from his, and so on, back to the philosophers themselves. Whenever I pointed to what seemed to be a contradiction in the received traditions—sharp differences between Ibn Sina and Ibn Roshd or Suhawardi on a certain point—he immediately reverted to what he called "The Tradition." And he appealed to "The Tradition" in order to resolve what, after all was said and done, he took to be nothing more than an apparent contradiction of slight importance. His sense of unbroken continuity with the remote past of his tradition was overwhelming.[4]

Most of us in the West, on the other hand, are shot through with historical consciousness, that is, with a sense of the gulf that separates us from our past and the speed with which the new distances itself from the old. We are convinced, therefore, of the need for careful, methodical reconstruction of the past. We feel called to test critically the evidence on which our putative knowledge of

---

4. I do not mean to imply that all Moslem scholars are traditional in this sense, since many of them are also possessed of historical consciousness; nor do I mean to imply that there are not deep insights gained by such a traditional sense of immediate continuity, insights that are difficult for, even perhaps not accessible to, critical-historical methods.

the past rests. This need for a bridge to the past accounts for the development of modern historiography, and for the considerable trust many place in historical-critical method. Even those who have grave suspicions regarding the uncritical use of the historical-critical method, especially in matters religious, approach the past with what can only be described as a "critical" attitude. What Paul Ricoeur has referred to as "the hermeneutics of suspicion" is abroad. Indeed, the Renaissance unmasking of medieval forgeries, such as the pseudonymity of Dionysius the Areopagite and the falsity of the Donation of Constantine, may be taken as prelude to the attitude that several centuries later fashioned the historical-critical method. What is more, some are caught between the double suspicion of the critical method on the one hand, and of the past itself on the other—lacking as they do the confidence of my traditional Moslem scholar. In such circumstances the perennial questions deliberately pose themselves anew, and ask for newly formulated answers. Now, the question: Why be moral? is just such a perennial question. What is more, in the present climate of hyper-criticism with its largely negative and sometimes destructive results, the possibility of a positive answer assumes fresh importance.

We must be precise, however. The question, Why be moral? is not strictly speaking a matter of ethics proper. At least, not if we understand ethics to be a branch of philosophy and/or theology that sets forth the specific principles and guidelines of right conduct (general ethics) and that examines specific obligations and their relation to one another in the formation of a system of conduct (special and applied ethics). Ethics presupposes that we have answered the question: Why be moral?, or at least that we have provisionally affirmed it, for ethics examines how we ought to act in order to be moral. The question: Why be moral? requires us to step back a half step into the background of conduct and to inquire into the very foundations of morality.

Karol Wojtyła takes just this half step in the *Lublin Lectures* and *The Acting Person*. In the latter work he explicitly says that ethics is important and indispensable to a moral education; but he also tells us that he is not writing an ethics manual. Rather, he is examining what he calls the domain of the "pre-ethical," though it is obvious that such a work holds implications for ethics.[5] When one steps back into the foundations of ethics, one steps back into the question of what it means to be human, so that the question, Why be moral? leads to the question, What is man? *The Acting Person* is, then, an inquiry into philosophical anthropology, although with an orientation toward axiology and ethics.

It is clear from the *Lublin Lectures* that, in addressing the question, Karol Wojtyła is conscious of thinking within the broad canvas of the history of so-called Western thought. The broader influences upon him include that of Aristotle and St. Thomas, St. Augustine and St. Bonaventure,[6] and, to be sure, that of St. John of the Cross, about whom he wrote his doctoral dissertation at the Pontifical University of St. Thomas Aquinas in Rome.[7] He is also conversant with the various versions of Thomism: the structured, traditional Thomism of Garrigou-Lagrange at the Angelicum; the transcendental Thomism of Joseph Maréchal at Louvain; the existential-historical Thomism of Etienne Gilson; the existential Thomism of Jacques Maritain; the "act" Thomism of Josef de Finance; the participatory Thomism of Cornelio Fabro; and, of course, with various Polish Thomists, including his own teachers

5. In her editorial introduction to *The Acting Person,* the English editor, Anna-Teresa Tymieniecka, notes that in this, "his central philosophical work, . . . the author stresses that his study is strictly anthropological, not ethical," though "it also has significance for ethics" (*AP,* p. xxi).

6. Josef Seifert has argued for a Bonaventurian influence in "Karol Cardinal Wojtyła (Pope John Paul II) as Philosopher and the Cracow/Lublin School of Philosophy," *Aletheia* (Irving, Texas: 1981); cited and commented upon by Rocco Buttiglione in *Il Pensiero di Karol Wojtyła* (French trans.: *La Pensée de Karol Wojtyła* [Paris: Communio/Fayard, 1984]).

7. *La Fede secondo S. Giovanni della Croce* (Rome: Angelicum-Herder, 1979) (Eng. trans.: *Faith According to St. John of the Cross* [San Francisco: Ignatius, 1981]) [Grondelski item 7].—Maliński, *Pope John Paul II,* p. 20, recalls that during the Nazi occupation, the layman Jan Tyranowski had introduced Karol to the works of St. John of the Cross and St. Teresa of Avila in the meetings of the circle of the "Living Rosary" in Cracow. Immediately after the war, Fr. Różycki, professor of dogmatic theology at the seminary in Cracow, suggested to Wojtyła that he write a doctoral thesis on the theological virtue of faith in St. John of the Cross (Maliński, *Pope John Paul II,* pp. 88–89).

and colleagues.[8] He is also conscious of the so-called *Nouvelle Théologie* with its patristic leanings. In a word, he has gathered into himself a comprehensive knowledge of the history of philosophy and of Catholic theology, with emphasis upon the current situation.[9]

Wojtyła's own work in philosophy is to be located more precisely among the various kinds of philosophical anthropology that populate the world of contemporary thought. Further, within the spectrum of philosophical anthropology, his analysis is to be situated within the broad tradition of Christian personalism that has flourished in our own century, largely under French Catholic sponsorship. This includes the personalism of Maurice Blondel with its emphasis upon action.[10] The spectrum of Catholic personalism also includes the socio-political personalism of Emmanuel Mounier, as well as the metaphysical personalism of Jacques Maritain and the concrete personalism of Gabriel Marcel.[11] But his work

8. Maliński, *Pope John Paul II*, p. 159, reports Wojtyła, now pope, as reminiscing: "I have never studied philosophy in a regular way, or attended a course of lectures." Despite the irregularity of his induction, however, there is no doubt that he soon mastered the essentials of the discipline, including a sound and detailed grasp of the whole course of the history of philosophy, with special emphasis on the foundations of ethics. He proved his competency both in his teaching and in his subsequent publications.—Maliński, *Pope John Paul II*, p. 47f., also reports the impact made upon the young seminarian by Fr. Wais's philosophical *Theodicy*, which, after difficult study of it, opened up a new world to him. And later, when he had been assigned to write a *Habilitationsschrift* (i.e., a dissertation fitting him to teach at a university), Maliński (p. 110) pictures Wojtyła pointing at the works of Max Scheler with the comment: "Look what I've got to cope with. . . . I can hardly make it all out, my German is poor, and there are a lot of technical terms I don't know how to translate. Do you know what I'm doing? . . . I've started to make a translation of the whole book—there's nothing else for it." Surely there is some consolation here for harried doctorands!

9. For an excellent account of Wojtyła's background and context, see George Hunstan Williams, *The Mind of John Paul II: Origins of His Thought and Action* (New York: Seabury, 1981). This book is a mine of useful information about the intellectual background and formation of Karol Wojtyła, especially for the non-Polish reader. It is helpful more generally, too, in providing the broad context of Polish intellectual life during Wojtyła's formative years.

10. In the *Lublin Lectures* of 1954–55, Wojtyła lists Blondel's *L'Action* as one of his sources (*LV* 104), though he criticizes Blondel for giving too much weight to the dynamic movement in the act of will and too little to its objective moment (*LV* 91). See the positive comments of John Paul II on the significance of Blondel, *Osservatore Romano*, no. 14 (6 April 1993), p. 4 (édition française).

11. Throughout the *Radiation of Fatherhood*, I find a special resonance

also bears a certain affinity with non-Catholic personalism, such as that of the Protestant Paul Ricoeur and the Jew Martin Buber, as well as some aspects of the thought of Emmanuel Levinas. Finally, he is one of a number of distinguished Polish personalists.[12] Fortunately for the English reader, these debts are duly noted in the footnotes of the English edition of *The Acting Person*. Wojtyła's thought defines itself most directly, however, in confrontation with the practical philosophy of Immanuel Kant and even more with Kant's phenomenological critic, Max Scheler.[13]

Wojtyła's project in the *Lublin Lectures* and *The Acting Person*, as well as elsewhere, is neither to reform nor to replace traditional Catholic philosophy; nor is it to produce a new hybrid of traditional metaphysics and contemporary philosophy.[14] I will argue that he endorses the general lines of the traditional metaphysics laid down by the great Catholic philosophers and theologians of the High Middle Ages, and that he sees in that metaphysics a secure understanding of the real order. His particular attention is drawn, however, toward our contemporary situation and to pre-

---

(whether intended or not) with the thought of Gabriel Marcel. Cf. Marcel's "Fatherhood as the Vow of Creative Fidelity" in *Homo Viator*.

12. Stanisław Kowalczyk, "Personalisme Polonais Contemporain," *Divus Thomas* 88, nos. 1–3 (1985), pp. 58–76, situates Wojtyła within the personalist spectrum and in relation to other Polish philosophers, such as Mieczysław A. Krąpiec, Józef Tischner, Mieczysław Gogacz, Wincenty Granat, Józef Pastuszka, Ludwik Wciórka and Kowalczyk himself. In relation to Vatican II, see Wojtyła, "Der Mensch als Person" in *Von der Königswürde des Menschen* (Stuttgart: Seewald Verlag, 1980), pp. 43–47, esp.: "Neither the concept *homo faber* nor even the concept *homo sapiens* is adequate in its purely functional significance" to grasp the true worth of the human person."

13. Wojtyła's "Habilitationsschrift" for the Faculty of Theology in Cracow (1953) is available in German translation: "Uber die Möglichkeit, eine christliche Ethik in Anlehnung an Max Scheler zu schaffen." It forms the central work in *Primat des Geistes. Philosophische Schriften* (Stuttgart-Degerloch: Seewald Verlag, 1980), pp. 35–197. (For the original Polish, see Grondelski, item 44, and related items, 46, 50, 61 [these are also available in *Primat des Geistes*], along with items 71 and 33.)—Mention needs to be made also of Wojtyła's recognition of the work of the phenomenologist Dietrich von Hildebrand, especially in regard to the latter's defence of the reality of values within a personalist context. See, for example, Wojtyła, *La visione antropologica della Humanae Vitae* (1978) (Ger. trans. in: *Von der Königswürde des Menschen*, ed. Juliusz Stroynowski (Seewald Verlag, 1980), n. 1, p. 201; see also *AP* n. 36, p. 308, and n. 50, p. 311.

14. See Williams, *Mind*, p. 196.

vailing currents of thought. Among them he finds especially prom-
ising the movement of phenomenology initiated principally by
Edmund Husserl around the turn of the century, and especially in
the form in which it was developed by Max Scheler. In Scheler's
emphasis upon love and its importance for the person, as well as
upon the role of imitation in ethical life, Wojtyła found an echo
of interest to Catholic thinkers. He was concerned to show how
Scheler's system stood in relation to Christian ethics.[15] He remarks, "Scheler was engaged above all with practical philosophy,
and in this respect he is for the modern phenomenological school
what Edmund Husserl was in the realm of theoretical philosophy."[16] Wojtyła had already found in the thought of Immanuel
Kant a profound respect for the human person as an end and value
who is not to be used merely as a means by other persons, groups,
or the state. He found in Scheler, however, a critic of the excessive
formalism of Kant.

Wojtyła's ultimate interest is practical, in the sense of moral.
But that interest is in no way narrowly defined. He seeks to penetrate to the very essence of the moral act and of ethical consciousness. To do this he realizes that he must take seriously the dramatic
shift that has taken place in Western thought since the late Middle
Ages. For there has been a deep fascination with and cultivation

15. "In his system Scheler emphasized in a special way the significance of love
for the person and the role of imitation of an ethical model (eines ethischen Vor-
bilds) for the whole ethical life (das gesamte sittliche Leben)" (Primat des Geistes,
p. 38). See also Das Prinzip der Nachahmung im Evangelium anhand der Quellen
der Offenbarung und das philosophische System von Max Scheler (Primat des
Geistes, pp. 265ff.).

16. See Wojtyła's later "The Transcendence of the Person in Action and Man's
Self-teleology," in Analecta Husserliana 9 (1979): 203–12, esp. p. 212, n. 8:
"Mention is due here especially to M. Scheler. Profiting by certain ideas of E. Husserl and F. Nietzsche, he created the well-known 'material ethics of value,' being
the most developed form of ethics presented by a phenomenologist. The views of
Scheler, as is well known, were later developed by N. Hartmann; D. v. Hildebrand
and others assimilate them creatively to Christian ethics and render them in the
spirit of realism." There follow two references to Wojtyła's own works of 1959
on Scheler and St. Thomas.—Contact with Roman Ingarden's phenomenological
realism occurred after Osoba i czyn had been completed (A.-T. Tymieniecka, AP
xiii); the footnotes of the English edition draw attention to a relation to Ingarden
that is not close and whose methodological affinities go back to a common source
in Scheler (AP 302/n. 8, 307/n. 29, 312–13/n. 59) [Grondelski, item 33].

of the inner character of human consciousness in modern times, quite unlike the religious journey within the soul.[17] The inner-directedness of much of modern thought is not to be confused with the interior movement of transcendence that has always animated and still animates the religious thought and prayer of Christians. Perhaps it is not too much to call the modern movement inward the "secularization of interiority." The religious journey within seeks to lay the prayerful soul before God, whereas the modern journey within seeks to find and test the self as the human foundation for certitude and the basis for evaluation.[18]

Now, this interiorization is not a preoccupation of philosophers alone—say, for Descartes who developed introspection, or for Hume who developed empiricism, or for Kant who developed critical idealism. Such philosophers have simply given a kind of conceptual signature to what others in their cultural era have expressed in different ways in literature and art, in psychology and anthropology, in ethics and religion. Wojtyła is confident that modern techniques and approaches, and above all phenomenology properly modified, can help us to explore the inner region of human experience. But these techniques must first be purged of their idealism and subjectivism and be brought into harmony with a realistic metaphysics.[19]

17. Such as in St. Bernard, *On the Song of Songs,* or in St. Bonaventure, *The Journey of the Mind to God.*

18. I have drawn the distinction in some detail between the traditional religious conception of interiority (in such figures as St. Augustine) and the modern secular conception of subjectivity (in such figures as Descartes) in "The Geography of the Person," *Communio,* English language edition, vol. 13, no. 1 (Spring 1986): 27–48. The modern emphasis is upon the psychological and epistemological, or—in the peculiarly modern sense defined by the post-Cartesian problematic—the ontological; whereas the traditional sense is governed by the religious and metaphysical interiority whose destiny is not the human subject but nothing short of God. Despite his use of modern techniques of analysis, Wojtyła has subordinated the modern path of introspection (which so often leads to idealism) to the age-old path of interiority (which carries us toward transcendence and toward God). It is noteworthy that the modern problematic is itself under criticism from Deconstruction. I will take up Wojtyła's further analysis of the modern shift in the last chapter.

19. In "The Person: Subject and Community," *Review of Metaphysics* 33, no. 2 (Dec. 1979): 273–308, esp. 277–78, Wojtyła remarks: "[T]he importance of consciousness for subjectivity . . . was not much developed in the scholastic tra-

In all of this, what comes home to Karol Wojtyła is the dignity of the human person.[20] We hear much today of human rights and personal freedom; but it is easy for those who move in Catholic intellectual circles to take the notion of the human person as something granted by most thinkers. In its fullest and richest meaning it is born of the great Church councils, and it has remained the central reality of Catholic metaphysics, morality, and spirituality; but beyond Christian circles it is by no means an uncontroverted notion. It would be naive to think otherwise.

Since the beginning of modern thought, about four hundred years ago, there have been repeated attempts to oust the notion of person from the central role in the characterization of what it means to be human, and to replace it either with a supposedly more "objective" and often materialistic notion of the individual or of the collective, or to make do with a more psychological notion of the human subject, such as the self, the mind, the ego, consciousness, or subjectivity. These attempts to redefine the human being have met with considerable success. To be sure, we can use different terms interchangeably in everyday speech, as though they all mean the same. We can speak indifferently of "person," "self," "ego," and "subject," with little tangible harm done. Still, their differences remain hidden within these terms, for language has a built-in memory of which the speaker may not be wholly conscious. And these differences carry through to deflect our at-

---

dition. . . . [S]ince the time of Descartes, consciousness has been absolutized, as is reflected in our times in phenomenology through Husserl. In philosophy the gnoseological attitude has superseded the metaphysical. . . . Especially, the reality of the person demands a return to the concept of conscious *being* [emphasis added]. This being is not constituted in and by consciousness; quite the contrary, it [i.e., being] constitutes both consciousness and the reality of human action as conscious." Thus, Wojtyła's critique is quite different from Hegel's critique of his modern predecessors; for, while Hegel criticized the particularity of the modern form of consciousness, he went on to absolutize it on a cosmic scale.

20. Cf. the work of Andrew Woźnicki, *A Christian Humanism: Karol Wojtyła's Existential Personalism* (New Britain, Connecticut: Mariel Press, 1980) and *The Dignity of Man as Person: Essays on the Christian Humanism of His Holiness John Paul II* (San Francisco: Society of Christ). Father Woźnicki and Father Francis Lescoe (Mariel Press) have been active in the study and publication of Wojtyła's thought in North America.

tention at crucial turns, and to redirect our concern along their own preferred and pre–established lines.[21]

Now, the term "person"—in the rich metaphysical sense given to it by the above-cited Catholic philosophers, has not received much favor in the mainstream of modern and contemporary philosophy. It is not Karol Wojtyła's intention in his inquiry, therefore, to begin with the classical metaphysical definition of person.[22] He intends, rather, to describe human action in such a way that it will be seen to manifest the reality of the person in and through his or her actions out of the living experience of those actions. Hence the Polish title: Osoba i czyn (Person and Act).[23]

21. See my "Selves and Persons: A Difference of Loves?" *Communio*, English language edition, vol. 18 (Summer 1991): 183–206.

22. Indeed, he finds the classical definition of Boethius correct but insufficient because it stresses the individuality of the human person and reduces or compares him with other things in nature, whereas the consideration of a human being as person points up the irreducibility and uniqueness of each human person. Nonetheless, both the reducible and the irreducible are required in any complete account of the human being. In "Subjectivity and the Irreducible in Man," *Analecta Husserliana* 7 (1978): 104–14, esp. 110, he remarks apropos of the traditional metaphysics of act and potency (*agere* and *pati*): "However, while explaining thus the dynamic reality of man, there remains each time . . . the respective 'experience lived through' [the German: *Erlebnis*] as an aspect not directly included in this metaphysical explanation or reduction, since it is an irreducible element. From the point of view of the metaphysical structure of being and action, and therefore from the point of view of the dynamics of man when he is conceived metaphysically, dealing with this element may seem unnecessary. We may acquire a sufficient understanding of man, of his action and of what occurs within him, also without it. For many centuries on such an understanding the whole edifice of anthropology and ethics was being constructed. But as the need of understanding man as an only and unique person grows, and especially as the need of understanding the personal subjectivity of man in the whole dynamics of action and occurrence proper to him keeps growing, the category of 'experience lived through' gathers meaning, and what is more, a key meaning. It is not only a question of metaphysical objectivization of man as the acting subject or the agent of his deed, but the chief aim of this is to show the person as a subject living through his own deeds and experiences, and thanks to all this, his own subjectivity. When this demand is made upon the interpretation of 'man in action' (*l'homme âgissant*), the category of 'experience lived through' (*Erlebnis*) must find its place in anthropology and ethics and, what is more, must to a certain degree take its place in the center of respective interpretations." Nevertheless, "the phenomenological method is in the service of transphenomenological cognition," i.e., knowledge of reality (113).

23. Stressing the strict link between the two terms, Wojtyła remarks in "The Intentional Act and the Human Act, that is, Act and Experience," *Analecta Husserliana* 5. (1976): 269–80, esp. 270: "There is no proper expression in English

Using contemporary techniques of interior analysis, Wojtyła hopes to lead us to a new appreciation of the same rich reality that has been at the center of Catholic thought for centuries; but he builds his approach in the *Lublin Lectures* by way of a retrieval of elements of Western philosophical thought about the nature of moral action and ethics.

～

Before turning to *The Acting Person,* which represents the culmination of his philosophical inquiry, it will be helpful to look back upon the series of lectures the young professor of ethics gave at the Catholic University of Lublin.[24] I have found the *Lectures* to be all but indispensable in unravelling some of the more cryptic passages in *The Acting Person.* It seems to me that not enough

---

for this notion [of 'human act']; it will be instructive to see how the same notion can be expressed in other languages. We may take, for example, the Polish word, '*czyn*,' and the German '*die Tat.*' They do not identify fully with the French '*acte humaine*,' or the Italian '*atto umano*,' which terms are literal translations of the Latin '*actus humanus*,' but not necessarily inclusive of the entire metaphysical depth of the latter term when it relates to the objectivization of the dynamism proper to man as person. The Polish term '*czyn*' seems to be equivalent in content to '*actus humanus*' just like the German '*die (menschliche) Tat*,' although in a different language form, more phenomenological. The shade of meaning in the term '*czyn*' is expressed in Polish through a distinct verb '*działać*' (the Latin equivalent being '*agere*'), also the noun '*działanie*' which expresses different kinds of activity, for which reason one speaks for instance of the activity of animals, whereas '*czyn*' indicates only the activity proper to man as a person. It contains all that St. Thomas expresses in his '*actus humanus*' as well as in his analyses of '*voluntarium*'."

24. In an illuminating *Vorwort* to the *Lubliner Vorlesungen* (hereafter *LV*), Tadeusz Styczen remarks that these *Lectures,* appearing as they have, twenty-five years after they were given, permit us—better than any other of Wojtyła's writings—to see Karol Wojtyła as a craftsman in his own scientific workshop (*LV* 24). They are preludes, yet they stand in their own right. In them Wojtyła shows himself to be "the master of those who learn humbly from others" (*LV* 17). The young philosopher "passes effortlessly from modern to ancient times and again from the medieval to the modern." Indeed, in order to come to grips with Scheler's analysis Wojtyła had to return to the ancients (*LV* 18). The *Lectures* are steps along a way that is not to be fully understood without the later works, ranging from *Love and Responsibility* (1960) through *The Acting Person* (1969), *The Family as Communio Personarum* (1974), *The Person: Subject and Community* (1976), and the works of his Pontificate, such as *Redemptor hominis* and *Dives in misericordia,* as well as the Wednesday talks on the theology of love. All of these form a *magna charta hominis,* "ethics as normative anthropology" (*LV* 23). I can only hope in the span of these lectures to highlight the outlines of Wojtyła's anthropology by attention to several key works and thereby to invite further study.

attention has been paid to them, at least in English, and that they outline the essentials of the problem that the young philosopher set himself. Even more, they set forth the lines of the solution at which he arrived and which he maintained in *The Acting Person.* Indeed, the later work is a refinement and re-ordering—according to different principles and a different approach—of the line of thought pursued in the *Lectures,* although the later work shows more subtlety of analysis and greater emphasis upon the inner, more subjective aspects of ethical experience.

The brief indication that follows cannot convey the vigor of the argument of these early lectures, their attention to detail and the more finely nuanced judgments—all carried on throughout more than four hundred printed pages. I will stress less the problem entered into[25] than the elements of the solution he draws from the thought of other philosophers in the twenty-five-hundred-year history of the discipline. I make no attempt to enter into a critical assessment of the various philosophical positions or to pronounce upon the accuracy and fidelity of Karol Wojtyła's understanding of them. I will say, however, that he evidences a careful reading of them, selective in accordance with his stated purpose.

The first of the three lecture series, given during the academic year 1954–55, is entitled *Act and Lived Experience* (*Akt und Erlebnis*). After sketching Scheler's ethics of value (*Wert*), Wojtyła passes on to Kant's ethics of duty (*Pflicht*). He stops to compare the two systems, and introduces some considerations raised by certain modern psychologists.[26] Finally, he passes on to an extended discussion of "the significance of the Aristotelian-Thomistic theory of potency and act for the structure of the ethical act" (*LV* 94).

In the preamble Wojtyła tells us that the empirical basis of philosophical ethics is ordinary human experience (*Erfahrung*) (*LV* 31). What is of absolutely primary importance for Wojtyła, however, and the aim of his reflection, is to show that this empirical total-

25. The problem had received its formal statement in his *Habilitationsschrift* presented to the Cracovian theological faculty in 1953. For the German edition, see *Primat des Geistes. Philosophische Schriften.*
26. Specifically, the work of N. Ach, J. Lindworski, and J. Reutt.

ity—the ethical life as lived experience (*Erlebnis*)—has in fact the structure of an act. The key notion in ethics is human action. To show further the importance of the notion of act or action, the author looks at a number of philosophical systems—and first of all at that of Max Scheler, who raised the notion of value to the first rank in ethics, and raised it directly over against Kant, who gave the primacy to duty.

This contrast between value and duty rests on a deeper disagreement. For Scheler grounds the ethical life—the lived experience of ethical values—in common experience, whereas Kant excludes ordinary (that is, sensory) experience from ethical life, and even opposes its role in ethical considerations (*LV* 31–32). What joins both philosophers together, however, in the opinion of Wojtyła, is their common failure to explain why ethical life and ethical science must find their proper form and structure in action. Four terms, then, have come into play: value and duty, experience (both empirical and lived) and action.

Wojtyła considers Scheler to have the advantage over Kant insofar as Scheler brings us directly to the essence of things as they are given immediately in experience (*Wesenschau*), whereas Kant leaves us only with appearances, with the structure of phenomena. Nevertheless, we are warned by Wojtyła that the essence of which Scheler speaks is a structure brought about by and within experience, a phenomenological structure. Scheler's ethical essence is not the being of which the (classical) metaphysician speaks. In their different ways, both Kant and Scheler present us with constructions from experience and within experience, yet constructions that do not touch the existential reality of the ethical life itself.

There are still other important differences. For Scheler, the bearer of ethical values is the human person, who undergoes them in lived experience; and this is undoubtedly true. According to Wojtyła, however, Scheler the phenomenologist is only interested in these values insofar as they form the content of the intentional acts of the human subject and its experience. Moreover, for Scheler, the human subject or person is not at all a substance, but is merely the subjective unity of these experiences. According to Scheler, concrete material values are given to us immediately in and through feeling (*LV* 37–38). Indeed, Scheler subordinates the will to feeling, and thereby reveals an inadequate grasp of the decisional character of ethical life. He understands ethical life in terms of lived-through emotional experience, instead of in terms of deliberately lived-out human action.

This subordination of the will is part of Scheler's resistance to Kant, who placed so much emphasis on the role of will in ethical life: the will to do one's duty out of respect for the moral law. Scheler, on the other hand, insists that "ethical experience must be cleansed of all elements of ought and duty." Wojtyła finds that Scheler has given too much to the role of felt experience in ethical life and too little to the role of the will in that ethical experience (*LV* 44). Wojtyła remarks that, in such a system as Scheler's, "the person as causal originator (*Urheber*) finds no place in the framework of phenomenological intuition. . . . The whole dynamic character of the being of the person is lost. . . . The person remains only the subject of experiences, and indeed is strictly a passive subject. On the contrary, [for Scheler] the person is not the originator of action, he does nothing" (*LV* 45). To be sure, this is far removed from Wojtyła's understanding of person as act.

Wojtyła's criticism, voiced in different ways, is important for understanding his own project. He finds that Scheler slights action (in favor of experience) precisely because he slights being in its realistic sense (in favor of consciousness). And so, Wojtyła turns to metaphysics, not out of piety toward a venerable tradition, but in order to retrieve the reality of act and in order to give to act the primary role within the entirety of the ethical life as it is lived and experienced. I venture to say that Wojtyła is not a metaphysician by calling, and that he is challenged immediately by the practical issues of life. Still, he too hungers after the truth of the way things are, and in order to give a more adequate account of the ethical life, this "ethicist of act" calls upon the metaphysics of being and its anthropology to explain how the human person emerges from being a passive subject of experiences to become a responsible agent of moral actions (*LV* 45).

Still, Scheler is not dispatched so easily nor without due thanks. For, if the person is the originator of his ethical actions, still we cannot ignore Scheler's demand that the fullness of ethical life must be made manifest in and from experience (*LV* 46–47). Scheler's ethics of value challenges us to explain why he does not take into account the full ethical fact as it is lived out in ordinary human experience: Why does Scheler not recognize as essential to moral value and to ethics the fact that we do good or evil, that we experience ourselves to be originators of ethical action, that we feel responsible for our actions, and that feelings of merit or guilt arise spontaneously within us? For, surely, they arise within us from our recognition of personal causality. This observation is not theory but plain human experience. These are the common facts of ethical life, and they should be included in the starting point of any ethical analysis.

Wojtyła suggests that Scheler employed a methodological reservation that prevented him from acknowledging the experience of the "I" as causal originator of ethical action. The reservation stemmed from several considerations. Scheler presupposed that causality is transcendent and therefore outside the analysis of experience to which phenomenology is devoted. Scheler's emphasis upon the emotional character of human life emphasized the passivity of the human subject and thereby reduced the active principle—that is to say, the will—to a mere epiphenomenon of the life of feeling within the totality of the ethical act. Moreover, Scheler rejected causal efficacy as part of his rejection of Kant's emphasis upon the performance of duty.

In truth, Wojtyła maintains, the process of willed ethical action is much richer than Scheler took it to be (*LV* 50–51). The failure to make proper room for the causal efficacy of the will prevented Scheler from recognizing the proper level of ethical life. For it is precisely voluntary causality that makes an act ethical—makes it morally good or bad. Wojtyła's point is that the very fact of causal efficacy is rooted in ordinary ethical experience. Once the methodological reservation against causality is removed, the role of the will and its causation become open to phenomenological analysis.

Now, it is to such causality that Aristotle and St. Thomas have given detailed attention. Scheler was so opposed to the formalism of Kantian ethics and so opposed to a normative ethics that he mistook for the whole of the ethical act what is only a part or moment of it—namely, the experience of feelings of value (*LV* 70–73). But it is precisely here that Aristotle's analysis of agency and St. Thomas's analysis of willed action become integral to Wojtyła's analysis of the ethical fact and to the understanding of ethical experience and ethical life. Their metaphysics, and the anthropology arising from it, are not merely extrinsic correlations to ethical analysis; nor are they merely supplementary or complementary to that analysis. Instead, their metaphysical anthropology is necessary and intrinsic to the analysis; it is an essential ingredient of an adequate account of the ethical fact taken in its fullness. *Qua* accounts, to be sure, metaphysical explanation and phenomenological interpretation differ in their aims, premises, and methods; but they meet in the same real base: they are united within the ordinary experience of moral life.

Unlike Scheler, Kant places the ethical realm in the will and its action (*LV* 74). But as with Scheler, Kant's ethics results from the way in which he construes experience. For Kant, the purely noumenal and a priori character of ethics results from his inability to derive metaphysics from experience (*LV* 55). Kant does stress action and will in his ethics, but it is the action of *homo noumenon*, and it remains immanent to the subject. Kant values freedom, but the idea of freedom remains a mere ideal postulate of pure reason (*LV* 56). The practical reason or will in Kant does engage the empirical order, but it engages the empirical order only inasmuch as the inclinations found there are to be brought to the moral order by means of the formal element of the subjective maxim that coincides with the moral law, that is, with the factor of universalizability (*LV* 62).

For Kant, the will is free only when it lives wholly and exclusively by and for its own inner law, independent of and indifferent to experience (LV 61). The quality of a moral act for Kant is not determined by any inclination of the will toward the goods encountered in experience. On the contrary, no inclination can provide the measure for the moral value of an act, since for Kant inclinations are empirical and even pathological (LV 58). Kant insists that morality demands self-determination, but its autonomy must be secured without empirical inclinations and even in opposition to them (LV 63). As a consequence, the human being in its fullness, by virtue of its empirical factors, is excluded from the ethical sphere, which belongs instead to the pure noumenal subject (LV 59). The empirical aspects of the human person bear upon the ethical sphere only insofar as the ethical norm issues from pure reason in the mode of a command, the pure and formal imperative of duty (LV 59).

Kant does admit one properly ethical emotion: it is the feeling of reverence for the law (LV 66). Kant can admit this because it introduces nothing heteronomous into the will, which retains its pure autonomy. Indeed, while obligation and duty remind us of a certain negative tension between reason and the appetites, reverence for the necessity of the moral law lends to duty a positive aura (LV 67). Nevertheless, both Scheler and Kant miss the proper domain of ethics. Scheler's ethics of value stems from his conception of the person as the passive subject of the feelings describable in the terms of his phenomenology, whereas Kant's ethics of duty is the product of his denial of a realistic metaphysics (LV 69).

Karol Wojtyła insists, however, that in reality both value and duty are parts of the total ethical experience. What is more, we are conscious of being moral agents; we actually experience our moral efficacy (LV 70). Of course, neither Kant nor Scheler sets out to deny such an experience or to deny the integrity of the ethical act. Yet, because of prior methodological decisions, each has failed to incorporate their privileged element into the totality of the concrete ethical act. Instead, duty and value each are made to claim the whole of the act, and so construed they must exclude one another; in truth, they are essential but partial aspects of an indivisible unity of ethical experience and action (*LV* 81).

What is lost in both philosophies is the unity and integrity of the moral act. With Scheler the formal element of reason is neglected in favor of feeling, and the felt material values are not incorporated into the action. With Kant the formal element in its purity is so stressed that the material content is excluded, and once again the unity of the ethical act is lost. With the loss of that unity and integrity, each account fails to explain how the whole person is perfected by moral action (*LV* 76–77). In a certain way, Scheler is closer to the integrity of the action than Kant—whose sense of obligation is more a criterion than a full-fledged experience (*LV* 78)—yet Kant is surely more correct in seeking the basis of ethical action in the will (*LV* 82).

The fateful question that must be asked of any ethics is: How does a person become good—or evil? Scheler provides no explanation of how values perfect a person, that is, how they complete that project which is the human person. This is because, if he does not actually separate the dynamic principle from the values, Scheler certainly subordinates it to them; but the values are taken to be mere intentional contents, the feelings or emotional materials of the experiencing subject (*LV* 71). Kant's pure duty, on the other hand, cannot perfect or complete the whole person either, since it eliminates the empirical factors from the ethical domain. At first sight, Kant's ethics promises to be more efficacious than Scheler's, because he recognizes the importance of the moral agent; but in effect the will's causality in Kant is all but absorbed into the formalism of the law as pure imperative norm (*LV* 90–91). In truth and in fact, however, contrary to both positions, value and duty do interpenetrate and condition each other in the ethical act, which is undertaken by the whole human person (*LV* 85).

And so Wojtyła turns to Aristotle's and Thomas's analysis of human action in terms of potency and act. Thomas has resolved the problem just because he has secured the appropriate place of the will in the structure of the human person. He has been able to do that because he has situated the human person in the wider context of being. Specifically, he has recognized the proper object of the human will: the good understood as the object of rational desire, that is, the good as submitted to the will in the light of reason (*LV* 92). Thomas's metaphysics shows us not only that we know in the context of being but that our willing is exercised in that same context. The turn to the metaphysics of being and the anthropology of personal being, then, is integral to the analysis of the ethical fact, precisely as the exercise of a motivated freedom, and so, precisely as ethical. Moreover, such an anthropology maintains the integrity of the whole human being. It does not divide, nor does it exclude, dimensions of the person (*LV* 90).

In attending to action as the focus of ethical life, Thomas is able to recognize the human person as both source or originator of the action and as subject or recipient of the action's effect. The effect, however, is unlike any other result. The question is: How is the ethical value bound up with the causality of the acting person (*LV* 94)? Wojtyła replies that it is bound up with the nature and structure of the human agent, precisely as human. The person, and not only the will, comes to be good or evil in and through ethical or unethical action. Ethical values are not only intentional contents of experience; they become real features of concrete persons (*LV* 95–96). The values of honesty and courage, through honest and courageous action, become an honest and courageous person.

The will is a constitutive factor of human nature and of the concrete human person. In its origins the will is a potentiality for the good. It is intrinsic to ethical life, not only because it is the power of free exercise, but also because it is a specifically rational factor in human nature and in the concrete human person. The reason submits different goods to the will in the light of the objective norms rooted in reality. The will is free to act according to the norms or against them, but reason does play a normative, that is, a norm-setting, role (*LV* 97).

More is needed, however, to understand why a person as a whole becomes good or evil through ethical actions. After all, the potentiality to think or to laugh is also part of what it means to be a human person; but whereas thinking and laughing may make us clever or amusing, they do not make us good or bad without qualification (*LV* 98). Other qualities may make us "good at" something, but not simply good overall. Why do ethical values alone perfect the person *simpliciter* and not merely in this or that aspect (*secundum quid*)? Karol Wojtyła answers: Because ethical values touch that which is specifically personal in human beings, namely, the very center of their freedom, a freedom that through the context of goods is ordered to the good of the specific possibilities of the person (*LV* 101). These are concrete possibilities for actual persons. Through the free and conscious exercise of the will, the being that is the good determines the being of the agent-person and brings about a real qualification of the person. It is Wojtyła's judgment that only a philosophy of being (such as that of St. Thomas) is able to give a basic account of the moral realization of the person (*LV* 102–3).

Having set out the problem as he sees it, and having suggested the outlines of his solution, Wojtyła clarifies and develops his reflections in the second and third series of lectures, entitled respectively "The Good and Value" (1955–56) and "Norm and Happiness" (1956–57). In them he integrates his project within the discourse of Western philosophy by means of a commentary upon aspects of certain ethical philosophers: Plato and Aristotle, Augustine and Thomas Aquinas, Hume and Bentham, Kant and Scheler. It is neither possible nor, for the present purpose, necessary to present his detailed and often insightful comments. It is enough to indicate how he fills in the background of his own analysis of ethical action.

First, he builds up the character of the good as he understands it. Plato had already seen that truth is intrinsic to the good, and he had also identified the good with perfect being. It was left to Aristotle, however, to correct Plato's metaphysical idealism (*LV* 125, 246). Aristotle understood the good to be the concrete goal of tendency and of action (*LV* 134). Ethical good is not grasped first and foremost as a norm (in the way in which Kant speaks of duty) but rather as a value able to complete and perfect the human being. The human being is meant to choose and to act according to virtue and thereby become nobler. Aristotle grounded the good life in the context of being, and he intended reason to safeguard the proper good of the human being (*LV* 148–52). Norms for the will and for action arise, then, out of the agreement of reason with being. But, unlike Plato, Aristotle does not conflate the good with truth. The norm is not identical with truth or the good; nor does the norm determine them by external obligation. Instead, for Aristotle, the norm is a function of reason that operates within both the order of being and the order of the good (*LV* 152).

Wojtyła finds in St. Augustine *qua* philosopher the joining of the doctrine of creation (first received from Revelation) with the Platonic notion of participation. Moreover, to possess the good is not enough; nor is virtue sufficient for the completion of the human person. One must also love the good, which is always bound up with real being (*LV* 159–61). What is more, for Augustine, as for Thomas, the absolute Good is God, Who is pure and actual Being and most perfect Happiness (*LV* 175).

Thomas Aquinas deepens the standpoint of Augustine, however, by wedding Augustinian participation to Aristotelian realism (*LV* 197, 245). But he goes beyond Aristotle, too, with his insight into the existential nature of the good (*LV* 197). Existence is the definitive feature that is constitutive of the good (*LV* 244). For Thomas, the good is good only insofar as it in some way actually exists: *esse actu*. Indeed, the more complete the existence of something, the more complete is its being, and thereby the greater is its goodness (*LV* 196). The absolute perfection of the good is rooted in *esse* as act (*LV* 177).

Karol Wojtyła draws the ethical implication of this actual identification of the good with being as existential act.[27] By virtue of its finality the good draws its power to perfect or fulfill the human

27. The influence of existential Thomism is manifest throughout these lectures and seems to derive largely from Joseph de Finance (*Être et âgir*); see *AP* 303, n. 11 and 307, n. 30. No doubt, the general influence of Etienne Gilson, Jacques Maritain, and Cornelio Fabro, along with Polish Thomists, is also present. Cf. R. Buttiglione, *Il Pensiero*, p. 169, n. 23, and G. H. Williams, *Mind*, p. 147 and pp. 371–72, nn. 8 and 15.

being, not from substance, form, or quality, but from this very actuality of existence (*LV* 178–79). Being itself strives for perfection through the good (*LV* 246). Wojtyła considers Thomas's most original teaching to be this development of the interrelationship between being, truth, and the good (*LV* 177). In contrast, neither Scheler, whom Wojtyła calls an essentialist, nor Kant, whom Wojtyła considers a formalist, can account for the real impact of ethical values upon the development of the human person (*LV* 214, 234–37). On the other hand, by recourse to more traditional philosophy, the Aristotelian concepts of act and potency are able to provide an account of the development of the human person through the actualization of his or her potentialities. And a metaphysical realism (such as that of St. Thomas) can give its account of the person and his or her knowing in terms of being.[28] At the same time, with the help of the notion of participation, Thomas's existential act can also account for how and why it is that the person actually becomes better or worse through the actualization of his or her personal being (*LV* 244–45).

Still, it would be misleading to present Wojtyła's defense of metaphysical realism without drawing attention to his insistence upon the distinctive character of the practical order, as it arises out of the convertibility of the true and the good in their being. It is here that he finds so helpful Thomas's subtle analysis of the dynamic structure of the will and its relation with the intellect. Wojtyła tells us that the perfection of the human person rests upon the will, which alone is—in the strict meaning of the word—decisive (*LV* 189).

Commenting upon Thomas, but without doubt appropriating the position for his own, Wojtyła continues the analysis of action. Form, he tells us, is the primary act that constitutes a being in its fundamental dynamism. Action, on the other hand, is secondary act that carries out that dynamism. Now, in a human being, will directs the person's act, and it is master of all properly human activity. Moreover, the will possesses an inherent potentiality to-

28. Recall the discussion of mere knowledge in *Our God's Brother* and *Radiation of Fatherhood*.

ward the good. This good, insofar as it completes the person who acts, is actualized in and through the person's action in accordance with the goal for which he or she strives (LV 189). Properly human acts are taken with deliberation and according to the level of the agent's knowledge of reality (LV 389), a knowledge that anticipates the value of the good in relation to the person (LV 412–13).

Against Scheler, Wojtyła remarks that it is not feeling but rather intelligence that can present a moral value as the antecedent norm of action: "the moral value anticipated by the intellect, and which the will of the person takes possession of, arises in each act out of the dynamism of the being of that person. It arises out of the relation between what he or she is to what he or she is [meant] to become" (LV 412). Each act enjoins the interplay of reason and will, so that in human action the truth plays a role along with the good.

Indeed, truth is normative for human action; but the truth that is normative for human action is not, strictly speaking, directly theoretical truth. Without denying the rich conception of *theoria* among the ancients, Wojtyła here seems to mean by "theoretical" the descriptive or elucidative truth of modern analysis. Such truth does, of course, play an indirect role in human action. But practical truth in the sphere of human action has its own distinctive character and order, for truth becomes practical when it presents some being or aspect of being as the goal of the will's activity and under the guise of the good. In the sphere of action, moreover, "practical reason grasps the good prior to grasping the object as being" (LV 182, 198). This perhaps surprising statement deserves attention. Here, indeed, is a practical thinker! That is, one who thinks about *praxis* from its own point of view.[29] Reason in its practical mode knows the truth, just as the same reason knows the truth in its theoretical mode, but in its practical mode it knows the truth from the viewpoint of action and the good (LV 180).

In view of the above affirmation of the priority of good in the

29. Cf. Wojtyła's remarks on praxis in: "Il problema del costituirsi della cultura attraverso la 'praxis' umana," *Revista di Filosofia Neo-scolastica* 69: 3 (1977) (also *Sapienza* 29: 4). *La filosofia di Karol Wojtyła* (Bologna, 1983) contains P. Pollini, "Il problema della filosofia della prassi in Marx e Wojtyła."

order of practical reason, we might ask whether Karol Wojtyła's anthropology commits him to a renewed Augustinian emphasis, perhaps even in the manner of St. Bonaventure? I would say, not quite. It seems to me that Wojtyła's understanding of the relation between being and the good stands closer to that of St. Thomas. If we remain at a general level and identify Being Itself in God as pure act, we have a doctrine common to both St. Bonaventure and St. Thomas; but we come upon a diversity of doctrine as we press further into the meaning and role of *esse* in each thinker.[30] We have seen Wojtyła insist that the Thomistic notion of existential act is necessary for a fully adequate account of human action. Moreover, action commands primary attention in Wojtyła's project. As eminently practical, action is ordered to the good. For Wojtyła, however, the good is not only rooted in being as existential act, it is convertible with being, and precisely with being as existential act (*esse actu*).

If that is so, then we must speak of the good as primary in the practical order without undermining the primacy of being in the most universal and most fundamental ontological order. The distinction between being and the good is only a conceptual distinction, but the approach of the theoretical reason differs from that of the practical reason, as the theoretical account differs from the practical.[31] It may be, then, perhaps implicitly, that Wojtyła's remark about the priority (not the primacy) of the good in the practical order opens a second general issue. Explicitly, we have seen that Wojtyła is seeking to introduce experience into the account of ethical action; but his distinction between priority and primacy suggests that his emphasis is placed precisely upon experience

30. See G. P. Klubertanz, "*Esse* and *existere* in St. Bonaventure," *Mediaeval Studies* 8 (1946), 169–88. In the *Itinerarium*, Bonaventure passes from a consideration of Being Itself, stressing the unity of the Divine Being in the sixth level, to a still higher level of contemplation, which is given over to the Divine Trinity and the Good. This is generally in keeping with the Dionysian and Neoplatonic insistence upon the primacy of the good.

31. It may be that this difference of approach and of account bears some affinity with Jacques Maritain's distinction between the theoretically practical and the practically practical.

practically ordered to the good which in turn is rooted in and convertible with being.

Now, despite the Thomistic insistence upon the analogical character of real being in which diversity overshadows likeness, the account provided by traditional metaphysics (as the science of all being as being) manages only to give its account of the good in terms of the universal and transcendental features common to being as such. The account situates the good in the context of being, and acknowledges the human good as proportioned to man taken as a distinctive mode of being. Man and the human good are interpreted as sharing the same transcendental features of all being, even though they share those features diversely. And so, because the convertibility of being and the good lies at the root of the theoretical and practical orders, their convertibility seals an identification that preserves the primacy of being, inasmuch as the good (which has priority in the practical order) is identified with being as absolutely primary.

Is it possible that Wojtyła provides an answer to this reduction of the good to being? No doubt, Wojtyła's anthropology is an anthropology of the good, the good that is convertible with being. If we ask: What is the distinctive character of the ethical action that is called forth by the good? Wojtyła tells us that it is freedom:[32] the good exercised by a freedom that is responsible to the truth of being. Or more precisely yet, the good is freedom as the essential mode of spiritual being. Wojtyła may be seen as seeking to articulate a concept of spirit, not simply as immaterial being, but as ordered to the distinctive good of being in the form of spirit. Freedom, then, is the good that is convertible with being as spirit. To describe freedom as the proper mode of spiritual being is to secure the realism that is an unshakeable objective of Wojtyła's anthropology. For Wojtyła, the being understood theoretically is transformed into the being grasped practically in ethical action.

---

32. If I am correct, then Wojtyła has here appropriated the primary value of much of German idealism with its emphasis upon freedom and spirit, while ensconcing it within a traditional metaphysical horizon.

In playing down action in favor of passive experience, Scheler is too little practical. But he is also too little metaphysical, since for him value is indifferent to existence (*LV* 225). On both accounts, then, Scheler is unable to generate an ethics (*LV* 410). In fact, however, Wojtyła tells us, we can generate a philosophical ethics only if we recognize that, in ethical conduct, the norm of ethical action is nothing but the truth presented to the will by practical reason. Now, such a truth is the truth concerning the good (*LV* 246). It is the truth concerning the good of the human person, and so it is truth under the guise of the human good. Such a truth is constituted by value.

Some realists are disturbed by the use of the term "value" in discussions of the good. Wojtyła uses the term in a realistic sense, however. For him, the term is shorn of its merely subjectivist sense. By the term "value," if I have understood him, Wojtyła means the good insofar as it offers itself to and for the integral being of the concrete person. The norm in the mind, then, proposes a truth that is constituted by the good and the authentic value of the good for the person.

While the order of action differs from the order of cognition, still the object as known becomes ingredient in the order of action. Theoretical cognition itself is implicated in the practical knowledge offered to the will, and any analysis of the whole ethical fact that begins in experience must acknowledge the relationship of theoretical and practical knowledge to moral action. Once that is acknowledged, Wojtyła is convinced that the ethical fact—the experienced ethical act as object of analysis—lies open to an account based upon the interconnection of truth with the good in being (*LV* 198, 238, 248). Once again, neither Scheler's nor Kant's philosophies of consciousness can provide such an account, since they cut off the true and the good from being. Only an account based upon a metaphysical philosophy of being can succeed (*LV* 234–37, 241, 389, 395, 406). Metaphysics, then, is not simply complementary to ethical analysis; neither is it merely supportive of that analysis. Metaphysics is necessary and intrinsic to ethical analysis, if we are to give an adequate account of ethical experience and ethical life. But in our day a reading of the interiority of ethical life as experienced is also needed, and that is a reading that classical metaphysics alone is not able to provide. It is to this phenomenological reading that we will turn next.[33]

33. While the experiential account itself is presented in the next chapter, the full reason why such an account is needed is not completely given until the last chapter.

CHAPTER III

In the Cracow Study
A Philosophy Matures

In the *Lublin Lectures* we have seen Karol Wojtyła insist that, if we are to provide an adequate analysis of concrete human action and of the ethical life as a whole, we must include in that analysis a metaphysics of being understood as existential act. Now, Wojtyła does not relinquish this position in *The Acting Person,* which appeared as *Osoba i czyn* in 1969,[1] a dozen years after his Lublin lectures. But he does provide his analysis with a more articulated attention to human subjectivity, and to the interior life of the person as moral agent.

I first came to appreciate the philosophical reputation of Karol Wojtyła during a visit to Poland in 1978. When the English edition of *Osoba i czyn* appeared a year or so later under the title *The Acting Person,*[2] I picked it up with some expectancy. Although the book made a certain impression upon me, it was not an entirely satisfactory one. Despite many years of professional philosophy, including the study of Thomism and phenomenology, I could not—in my admittedly casual perusal—make out the lines of the argument or reach a conclusion as to the value of the results. I could not quite decide what the author was up to. I did not then know of the convoluted and slightly comical history of the edited

1. Polskie Towarzystwo Teologiczne (Cracow, 1969).
2. (Dordrecht, Holland: Reidel) in the series *Analecta Husserliana* 10 (1979). Translated by Andrzej Potocki; definitive text established by the editor Anna-Teresa Tymieniecka in collaboration with the author. The English-language editor mentions that the first half of the Polish text had undergone "thorough revision" in consultation with the author, but that the second half did not receive close scrutiny by the author, and that—due to his new responsibilities as pope—the author was even unable to proofread the last chapter.

English text, which had been revised with the rather heavy hand of a collaborator-editor. Still, I must admit that I was somewhat puzzled to find two seventh chapters at the end of the book, each containing more or less the same material in two separate versions, the latter in an appendix entitled "Literal Translation of Chapter Seven Prior to Editorial Revision." The very title of the appendix itself, as well as the need for an appendix containing the material of chapter seven, seemed to me something of a comment on the preceding seven chapters.

Indeed, at its appearance the English edition received some harsh criticism, caused in part perhaps because of its self-description, approved of by the author, that it was now the "definitive" edition.[3] Jean-Yves Lacoste[4] characterizes the English text as a disagreeable sort of "targum"—in other words, a rather poor paraphrase of the original. One would think that that was a severe judgment rendered upon any text. But Georges (Jerzy) Kalinowski[5] takes Lacoste to task, on the grounds that Lacoste overestimates the possibility of using the English text at all; to substantiate this assessment, Kalinowski provides details from Feliks Bednarski's list, by no means exhaustive, of the numerous and serious divergences from the Polish text.[6]

3. In the first preface the author speaks of "some changes which have been incorporated into the definitive version with the full approval of the author" (*AP* ix). In the "Translation of Handwritten Draft of the Author's Preface . . . to [the] English/American Edition of *The Acting Person* in *Analecta Husserliana*," the translation by M. K. Dziewanowski reads: "I thank the editor, Professor A.-T. Tymieniecka, who, guided by her excellent knowledge of the philosophic environment of the West, gave to my text its final shape. In comparison with the first and only Polish edition, the text now published in *Analecta Husserliana* contains a number of changes, although the basic concept of the work has remained unaltered" (*AP* xiv).
4. "Verité et liberté: Sur la philosophie de la personne chez Karol Wojtyła," *Revue Thomiste* 81, no. 3 (1981): 586–614.
5. "Autour de 'The Acting Person,'" *Revue Thomiste* 82, no. 4 (1982): 626–33.
6. See especially ibid., p. 628, n. 7, and p. 633, n. 18bis.—Lacoste continues the discussion in the same issue, pp. 634–44.—Cf. R. Buttiglione, *Il Pensiero di Karol Wojtyła* (Milan: Jaca, 1982), p. xiii, and pp. 141–42, n. 1. Buttiglione also cites A.-T. Tymieniecka, "A Page of History or from *Osoba i Czyn* to *The Acting Person*," *Phenomenology Information Bulletin*, no. 3 (October 1979): 3–52. Buttiglione's *Il Pensiero* makes use of the corrected manuscript text of the second

I should remark, in all fairness, that the footnotes added to the English edition are helpful in providing some context for the non-Polish reader.[7] But there can be no doubt that part of the difficulty encountered by a reader of the text of the English edition derives from its overly technical revision, more precisely, from the frequency with which the editor, by differing paraphrases of scholastic Latin terms, has supplanted an older technical language for another more contemporary one, thereby nudging the text in the latter direction. And so the English revision obscures the continuity of the author's thought with older traditions of thought. This is especially unfortunate in that it misleads the English reader regarding the relationship the author maintains between traditional metaphysics and contemporary phenomenology. In particular, it obscures the vitality which the author still finds in the intellectual traditions of medieval scholasticism, especially in the thought of St. Thomas Aquinas.

He has expressed his conviction regarding the continuing rele-

---

Polish edition, translated by Stanisław Dziwisz.—I wish here to acknowledge a special debt to the Rev. Dariusz Śleszynskí. During the passage of many hours, he patiently dug out for me the relevant portions of the Polish text so that together we might compare them with suspicious renderings in the first English edition. He has also identified key Polish terms and discussed them with me. I have included some of these in the text for those who may wish to check the Polish edition. Any misunderstandings are, of course, my responsibility.—I should note that I have also had access to a corrected version of *The Acting Person* in which the corrections have sought to increase the fidelity to the Polish text. In this corrected version, the reference (at *AP* xxiii) to the inability of the author to review the latter portion of the work is withdrawn. Moreover, the original translation of the seventh chapter (very slightly emended) replaces the seventh chapter of the first English edition. The use of the corrected English text has simply sharpened my critical awareness that the present text of the first English edition (*AP*) is, on the one hand, gravely misleading in important passages, and, on the other, because of an unstable rendering of important technical terms, simply muddled. The publication of a new edition is imperative.

7. Since the footnotes are not present in the first Polish edition, I had assumed that they might be the work of the English editor, but she has assured me in conversation that they were largely the work of the author. In any event, they need to be consulted in any serious study of the work.—In view of the critical reception of the English language edition (*AP*), a criticism which I share, it is only appropriate and just to recognize the valuable contribution made by Anna-Teresa Tymieniecka in publishing a number of articles by Karol Wojtyła in *Analecta Husserliana* during the 1970s and to which I have had recourse. These made his philosophy somewhat accessible to English readers before the appearance of *Osoba i czyn* in translation.

vance of St. Thomas on many occasions; nor are his remarks a mere formality. Thus, he points to St. Thomas's respect for the integrity of things and to the amplitude of the philosophy of being when it is centered in *actus essendi*. He admires the saint's preoccupation with the rational search for truth.[8] In an article in the *Analecta Husserliana*[9] he has written:

> Although I have arrived at the concept of the "human act" within the framework of a phenomenological inquiry of Husserlian orientation, it has to be pointed out that it coincides with the notion of "*actus humanus*" as elaborated by Thomas Aquinas. "*Actus humanus*" follows from the nature of the acting person, from man understood as subject and author of his action. Indubitably the most valuable element in Thomas's concept of "*actus humanus*" is that it expresses the dynamism of a concrete being, man in its specific complete determination drawn from the total man. That specific dynamism finds further elaboration in Thomas's studies of "*voluntarium*," for dynamism proper to the activity of man (*agere humanum*) and to the human act (in German it is expressed best through *die menschliche Tat*) finds its roots in the will. St. Thomas analyzes the nature, structure, and actualization of the will very much in detail.

Now, it is the view of Wojtyła himself that the metaphysics of St. Thomas Aquinas, however accommodated to the present situation, is an indispensable ingredient in ethical analysis, and so a textual revision in translation that obscures that ingredient poses a serious problem. For such a revision makes it difficult, if not impossible, to grasp the author's project in its entirety. It is ironic that, whereas Wojtyła has complained that Scheler and Kant have left out factors necessary to the analysis of moral action, so much more ought a reader to complain if a necessary factor has been obscured in the English translation of Wojtyła's own thought.

There can be little doubt that Karol Wojtyła was a dynamic classroom teacher; nor can one doubt the exceptional affection his students had for him, who seemed to be at once mentor, confessor, foster father and friend to many of them. But *Osoba i czyn* is a

8. On the occasion of the centenary of *Aeterni Patris*: "Discours de S. S. Jean-Paul II sur l'actualité de saint Thomas," in *Revue Thomiste* 80, no. 1 (Jan.–Mar. 1980): 5–12.

9. "The Intentional Act and the Human Act, that is, Act and Experience," *Analecta Husserliana* 5 (1976): 269–80; precisely at 279, n. 2.

difficult work, much more difficult than the *Lublin Lectures*. At the time of my first acquaintance with *The Acting Person* I had not yet heard the wry remark that was making its rounds at the Catholic University of Lublin.[10] Karol Wojtyła, it was said, had written the original Polish work ten years earlier, with full fore-knowledge that he would one day be pope and that he would then require it as reading for priests in purgatory. Now, if that was said of the somewhat less complicated Polish text, the English revised translation must be reserved for those in even lower depths and deeper trouble.

And so, the difficulty does not reside entirely in the English translation alone. The work itself is not meant for casual reading.[11] It demands study and, in my opinion, repays study.[12] Nevertheless, part of the difficulty stems from the intrinsic condition and nature of the work itself, even in its Polish original. The work is somewhat programmatic and frequently intuitive. There are leaps from one insight to another that need to be filled in; and there are sugges-tions thrown out to the reader that require further elaboration.[13] Nor should we be surprised. The author was an active professor at the Catholic University of Lublin only from 1954 to 1958, when he was made auxiliary bishop of Cracow.[14] Had he remained a professor of ethics—not a fate worse than death, after all—he un-doubtedly would have developed and refined the analysis further

10. Told by G. H. Williams, *The Mind of John Paul II: Origins of His Thought and Action* (New York: Seabury, 1981).

11. See, for example, the somewhat anguished though conscientious review by Joseph Pappin III in *The Thomist* 45 (1981): 472–80, esp. 472.

12. Once again, I express my appreciation to my sometime colleagues at the Cambridge Center for the Study of Faith and Culture, whose common discussions at the Center helped me through some of the thicker passages and the more obscure concepts of the work.

13. R. Buttiglione, *Il Pensiero*, p. 346, concludes that the work of Wojtyła re-mains incomplete in many aspects.

14. Nominated on July 10, 1958, and consecrated suffragan bishop on Sep-tember 28 of the same year. Incidents in his career that have received published notice may be found in the Polish-Italian bibliography by Wiktor Gramatowski and Zofia Wilińska, *Karol Wojtyła w Świetle Publikacji/Karol Wojtyła negli Scritti: Bibliografia* (Vatican City: Libreria editrice Vaticana, 1980). It should be noted, however, that even as bishop in Cracow, Karol Wojtyła maintained contact with the university in Lublin.

in academic philosophical argument.[15] He was called to another service, however, in which he has developed these same central insights, though in quite another style, and to the profit of a larger circle.

Given the relative isolation of the rich Polish intellectual life from that of North America, I myself might never have read *The Acting Person*; nor would you perhaps be interested in my reflections on it. Was it not the ancient philosopher Democritus from the remote provincial town of Abdera who replied to an upstart Athenian that, while he Democritus would not have been famous had he not come to Athens, his critic had managed to remain obscure even though he had been born and lived his whole life in that famous city? So too, we might not have known of the work of a Polish philosopher from Wadowice had he not come to Rome. But called he was, and come he did, and his writing has received added importance.

This brings me to the chief source of the intrinsic difficulty in the nature of the work itself: given time to study it, I have come to see that something rather new, something original is being proposed in it. Its novelty consists in the wedding of new methods of reflection with older, pre-modern traditions. Or rather, it is not the proposal itself that is so new, but the manner in which its resolution is carried out in the domain of the foundations of ethics. For the analysis manifests a philosophically sophisticated mind that is original and probing. Moreover, the work contains implications for theology, as well as for personal existence and communal life. It launches a serious and timely momentum of thought, even though not in a completely elaborated form. It is this originality that I should like to focus upon. And it is this feature that has led me to recognize that the book repays a patient scrutiny.

∽

The two prefaces by the author, as they appear in the first English edition, seem to strike a different tone from that of the *Lublin*

15. *Osoba i czyn* stirred up a lively discussion, however, and along with other discussions resulted in a colloquium held at the Catholic University of Lublin in 1970. In his remarks, Wojtyła expresses the hope that others will develop the line of thought in the work [see Grondelski, item 78].

Lectures, and may even seem to contradict my insistence upon the importance of the metaphysical element in Wojtyła's thought. He writes: "Granted the author's acquaintance with traditional Aristotelian thought, it is however the work of Max Scheler that has been a major influence upon his reflection" (*AP* viii). What is more, Wojtyła claims that his presentation of the problem is "completely new in relation to traditional philosophy," and is "an attempt at reinterpreting certain formulations" of St. Thomas's philosophy (*AP* xiii–xiv). Yet, even in the first English edition there is no evidence that he abandons, nor, if I have grasped his understanding of the issue correctly, could he abandon the metaphysical ingredient. This remains true, despite the systematic depreciation of the references to traditional philosophy and its vocabulary in the text of the first English edition (*AP*), which often simply replaces the Latin terms with different English paraphrases or leaves them out altogether. These editorial paraphrases obscure the meaning intended by the author's deliberate and constant use of the same technical term; for in the Polish text these technical terms are meant to serve as a shorthand reference to one or another traditional metaphysical concept or philosophical position.

In the same place, however, Wojtyła strikes a balance when he writes: "The author of the present study owes everything to the systems of metaphysics, of anthropology, and of Aristotelian–Thomistic ethics on the one hand, and to phenomenology, above all in Scheler's interpretation, and through Scheler's critique also to Kant, on the other hand (*AP* xiv)." Those who protest that Wojtyła is not constructing a new hybrid metaphysics are undoubtedly correct; but what is new is the way in which the project realizes itself by a mutual fructification of the two approaches, making, not a new ontology or metaphysics, but a new and integral account of personal reality as the latter is disclosed in human action.

Nevertheless, most English readers, dependent for the most part upon the first edition of *The Acting Person* and unaware of the author's stringent critique of Scheler as well as of Kant, may be misled in two respects. First, the reader may give too positive a weight to the part played by Scheler in Wojtyła's thought; secondly, the reader may relate metaphysics and phenomenology within Wojtyła's complete thought in too external a way. The *Lublin Lectures,* on the other hand, show the indispensable and intrinsic, yet ultimately insufficient, role that metaphysics plays in the analysis of the whole ethical act. Once the reader is alerted to Wojtyła's discussions in the *Lublin Lectures,* however, the reader is more likely to discover references to the intrinsic presence of metaphysics in *The Acting Person.* Still, given the cloud under which the first edition (at present the only readily available English edition) suffers, it is not easy to determine precisely the degree to which Wojtyła has, since his Lublin years, upgraded the part played by phenomenology within the whole enterprise.[16]

It seems to me beyond doubt that the metaphysics of being and the anthropology of the person retain their intrinsic and existential force in Wojtyła's philosophy of action, even as he explores in more detail, intimacy, and depth the interiority of the person as agent. Metaphysics and phenomenology differ as accounts; in terms of their own specific discourse they are more or less complete in themselves. But Wojtyła brings these two accounts to meet in a common work, so that he might give a more adequate total account of the integral fact of concrete personal action. By this interplay of accounts he hopes to explain a fact that is open to ordinary experience as well as to learned discourse with its several special accounts.[17]

Now, it is just here in the lived experience of the ethical act that phenomenology provides Wojtyła with a technique for methodically uncovering the inner life of consciousness. Beginning with insight into certain structures operative in human action, Wojtyła attempted by careful analysis to interpret them in such a way that the unity and complexity of experience, along with the physical and psychological dynamisms of the whole human person, are brought together in action. It is the aim of the analysis to manifest the reality of the human person as a free and responsible agent.

16. The helpful articles in *Analecta Husserliana* that appeared in the 1970s do not of themselves quite settle this issue, since they are addressed to what is primarily a phenomenological readership.

17. "The Intentional Act and the Human Act," pp. 274–75.

Still, much as phenomenology provides a technique for analyzing experience, in the contemporary current of idealism it has tended to turn human consciousness into a self-sufficient absolute. Wojtyła reminds his readers, however, that in reality the human person is not simply a consciousness. It is just here in this reminder that we can see the value of keeping in touch with metaphysics, since metaphysics places the human being in a context of real beings. It recognizes the human person both as physical and as spiritual, as both object and subject. We are forewarned, therefore, that the phenomenology at work in *The Acting Person* is a modified phenomenology with a realist intent. It is a phenomenology bent upon keeping in touch with the whole person as a distinctive being among other beings, even as it opens doors to the inner experience of the human agent.[18]

Because action draws together all of the elements in the experience of the person, the focus of the descriptive analysis is not consciousness but action. Moreover, the basis and source of action is not consciousness but rather the whole person, or as Wojtyła says, "man-acts" (*człowiek działa*). The whole person is caught up in and fully engaged through his or her own action. Instead of beginning with a notion of the agent and moving from that to the agent's action, Wojtyła proceeds along the reverse direction, so that "action reveals the person (*AP* 11).[19] Throughout the study,

18. Ibid., 269. Wojtyła, entering the discussion, says: "Undoubtedly the introduction of the notion of 'intentionality' as the key notion for the explication of the basic structural network of man as being-in-the-world is a crucial point of the phenomenological investigation. . . . However, this rational grasp of the otherwise opaque flux of man's consciousness is possible only at the level of the eidetic insight. . . . Through the intentional network we grasp the universal system of man as an individual, but can we do justice to man as a person? The rational, intentional act is the basic factor, which carries the essential lines of our operations securing the rationale of man as man; is it not the will which is the basic factor of human action through which man works out his concrete life? But 'action' contains as its root factor the act of deliberation and decision. I have attempted to show in my work that this fctor draws upon the complete organization of the individual's personality. Although it possesses also the rational intentional structure, it is not to be reduced to the intentional act no matter how complex."—In a moment we will meet with an even more radical decentering of intentionality.

19. If this were meant to contrast metaphysics and phenomenology, and to suggest that metaphysics is, if not simply a deductive science, then at any rate one that

if I am correct, the phenomenological analysis of interior experience is kept in interplay with the metaphysics of real being. The subject and source of experience is the whole human person; but the decisive center of human action is to be found in consciousness, indeed, in self-consciousness of a distinctive sort.

∿

For purposes of analysis, and by a method of bracketing, Wojtyła disengages consciousness (świadomość) as an aspect, so that he may consider it through itself (AP 13, 19–20).[20] The term "as an aspect" is meant to bring out the relative character of the analysis, that is, the relation of consciousness to other factors in the whole person; it is also meant to stand in contrast to the idealistic term "absolute," which treats consciousness in a nonrelative way (AP 29–30).

Now, Wojtyła's operation of bracketing resembles an algebraic function more than it does Husserl's Einklammerung; just as his discussion of induction (AP 14–15) is Aristotelian rather than empiricist. Moreover, his use of the terms "reduction" (AP 78, 82), "interpretation," and "understanding," take their meaning from his distinctive use of them in the analysis that follows (AP 15–18).[21]

---

proceeds solely by demonstratio propter quid, I would have reservations; but the present remark can be read without such a general contrast. It should be stressed here (as Stanisław Grygiel has pointed out to me in conversation) that the contrast, presumably between metaphysics and phenomenology, is not so much a contrast between traditional metaphysical explanation and phenomenological description as it is a concentration upon human action. And so, we ought not to forget that what interests Wojtyła is not principally a general metaphysics of being, or even of existential act, but that metaphysics insofar as it is focused upon and plays a role in the analysis of human action.

20. Wojtyła describes his approach "by analogy to operations used in algebra—as the placing of a term before brackets. We place outside brackets those factors of an algebraic expression which in one way or another are common to all the terms of the expression, that is, which are somehow common to everything that remains within the brackets" (AP 13). This operation of bracketing—which is not quite that of Husserl's—is not meant to exclude the common factor, but rather to disclose its otherwise hidden presence among the elements within the brackets.

21. See his discussion of phenomenological reduction (as "the operation in which is realized the fullest and simultaneously the most essence-centered visualization of a given object") and metaphysical reduction (which "leads to the full integration of nature in the person") (AP 79–82, emending "moment" to "oper-

To be sure, both he and Husserl seek to isolate a certain essence or *eidos*. But the very meaning of essence differs. If Husserl puts traditional metaphysics (as he understood it) out of play, Wojtyła does not. For Husserl *eidos* is a structured content of experienced givenness (*leibhaft selbstgegeben*), while for Wojtyła essence is the modality of a being of a certain sort: the human person revealed through action. The notion of being as existential act, understood in the most comprehensive and intensive way, permits Wojtyła to keep the doors of consciousness open to the whole of reality and to the entirety of the ethical act. And so, there is an entirely different fundament presupposed. Wojtyła does not suspend the factor of existence, nor does he put out of play the whole fabric of metaphysical principles, and above all, the principle of causality. Rather, for Wojtyła, to place something before brackets (*nawias*) is to put a certain factor in play in a prominent way, and, in this sense, it is an inclusive operation. Bracketing for Wojtyła is an operation that takes one aspect of an integral being and, by placing it outside the bracketed totality, permits us to examine the totality by the way in which the aspect affects everything in that totality; the aspect that is placed before the brackets thereby receives enhanced power to illumine everything that remains within the brackets. The totality with which Wojtyła is concerned is the integral human reality; the aspect under which he wishes to consider that reality is the aspect of "consciousness as such" (*AP* 29–31).[22]

If I have understood a particularly difficult part of the text, the analysis subsequent to the bracketing now yields subtle distinctions within the field of consciousness. But already, and from the

---

ation").—For an interpretation of the ethics of Wojtyła/John Paul II that attends to the question of method, see Carlo Caffarra, "Verita ed ethos dell'amore coniugale," in *Verita ed ethos del'amore coniugale in Giovanni Paolo II: Atti del I Convegno sul Magistero Pontificio (Ariccia, 25–27 mar. 1983)* (Milan: La Traccia), pp. 19–41, esp. pp. 19–23, where, in a discussion of method, Msgr. Caffarra underscores three concepts of an "adequate anthropology," viz., "reduction," "the integrity of the human person," and the "essentially human experience."

22. In "Subjectivity and the Irreducible in Man," *Analecta Husserliana* 7 (1978): 107–14; on p. 111, he writes of "a methodological operation which could be defined as 'dwelling upon the irreducible'" and which he identifies as personalistic.

beginning, Wojtyła has insisted that consciousness is not, as idealism would have it, an autonomous subject and the source of action. On the contrary, it is the man, the human person, who acts in the full and concrete sense, and not consciousness.[23] Once again, Wojtyła affirms his realism. In the opening preface to *The Acting Person* he had already written:

Our approach runs also counter to another trend of modern philosophy. Since Descartes, knowledge about man and his world has been identified with the cognitive function—as if, only in cognition, and especially through knowledge of himself, could man manifest his nature and his prerogative. And yet, in reality, does man reveal himself in thinking or, rather, in the actual enacting of his existence?—in observing, interpreting, speculating, or reasoning . . . or in the confrontation itself when he has to take an active stand upon issues requiring vital decisions and having vital consequences and repercussions? In fact, it is in reversing the post-Cartesian attitude toward man that we undertake our study; by approaching him through action (*AP* vii–viii).

And now, in carrying out this relativization of consciousness, and before entering into the distinctions which he draws within the field of consciousness, Wojtyła is at pains to deny that *intentionality* is the hallmark of consciousness in its entirety and, so to speak, its essential property.[24] The denial needs to be stressed. Wojtyła does not hesitate to go against the trend of much contemporary philosophy by insisting that consciousness in its general nature is not intentional. The denial of the identification of consciousness with intentionality is once again and paradoxically the emblem of Wojtyła's phenomenological realism. In view of the heavy, almost exclusive emphasis upon intentionality in phenomenology and much of contemporary philosophy (even since Kant),

23. Cf. Aristotle's insistence in the *De Anima* that it is not the eye that sees or the mind that knows, but rather the man who sees with his eyes and knows with his mind.

24. Wojtyła is careful not to ascribe intentionality as the defining feature of all consciousness; it is rather, a function of cognition within the field of consciousness. In this way, he preserves the realistic posture of consciousness and avoids attributing to the whole of consciousness the active constitution of the objects of which it is conscious. That way leads to idealism. These cognitive objects are "in the actual field of consciousness" and held "in the light" of consciousness, which does not constitute them; as we will see, it only mirrors them (*AP* 33).

the vigor with which Wojtyła presses his denial may seem startling, but the denial itself is of capital importance for grasping his anthropology. Cognition is intended to serve consciousness, which in its turn finds its fulfillment in action.

In this context, the denial of the primacy of intentionality operates within Wojtyła's analysis to uncover several other functions within the field of consciousness. But first the author acknowledges the proper role of intentionality in respect to consciousness. He ascribes intentionality to the cognitive function within the field of consciousness. Admittedly, cognitive activity is intentional. Cognition does indeed consist in the experience of other things: cognitive activity is always directed toward something other than itself. It is always concerned to penetrate some object and to constitute it as an object before the mind. This cognitive dynamism includes seeing, hearing, and other forms of perception, as well as conception (in the form of insight or induction), interpretation and explanation (in the form of reduction), and finally, judgment (*AP* 32, 303–4).

But Wojtyła insists that the cognitive function within the field of consciousness, by which the objects of cognition are constituted through intentional acts, not only does not exhaust consciousness—it does not even define the nature of consciousness in its concrete, existential reality. In effect, Wojtyła reverses the usual modern order between consciousness and cognition. Far from deriving the other aspects of consciousness from intentional acts of cognition, Wojtyła insists that these latter acts do not comprise the essential nature of consciousness but, on the contrary, only serve it. Or, as we have just seen in the quotation from *The Acting Person* (*AP* vii–viii), he has asked rhetorically: Is man revealed in thought, or in action? And if in action, then thought in the form of intentional cognition serves the concrete reality of the human person in act; it does not constitute that reality. Instead, Wojtyła suggests that what is proper to consciousness as such is its mirroring function: consciousness does not actively constitute the objects of cognition and their meanings, but it does reflect them.[25]

25. "It lies in the essence of cognitive acts performed by man to investigate a

Wojtyła calls consciousness in its mirroring function "reflecting consciousness" (*AP* 32, 303–4). It is most important, therefore, to understand that according to Wojtyła this reflecting consciousness is not derivative from the active dynamism of cognition. Cognitive objects are constituted in consciousness, but not strictly speaking by consciousness as such, that is, as experienced.[26] Rather, he tells us, "consciousness as such is restricted to mirroring what has already been cognized" (*AP* 32).

Now, the mention of "mirroring" puts one immediately in mind of the medieval Latin sense of *speculum, speculari,* and *specula-*

---

thing, to objectivize it intentionally, and in this way to comprehend it. . . . The same does not seem to apply to consciousness [as such]. In opposition to the classic phenomenological view, we propose that the cognitive reason for the existence of consciousness and of the acts proper to it does not consist in the penetrative apprehension of the constitutive elements of the object, in its objectivization leading to an understanding which constitutes the object. Hence the intentionality that is characteristic of cognitive acts—to which we owe an understanding of the objective reality on any of its levels—does not seem to be derived from acts of consciousness. These are not essentially intentional by nature. . . . Consciousness as such is restricted to mirroring what has already been cognized. Consciousness is, so to speak, the understanding of what has been constituted and comprehended [by cognition]. The purport of the preceding remarks is that the intrinsic cognitive dynamism, the very operation of cognition, does not belong to consciousness" (*AP* 32).—Scheler had already noticed the non-intentional character of certain psychic states of feeling (although Manfred Frings, *Max Scheler* [Pittsburgh: Duquesne University Press, 1965], p. 65, notes a certain inconsistency in Scheler on this point; see his subtle resumé, pp. 60ff.); but in any event this restricted recognition of the non-intentional character of some feelings is not at all the outright defense of the non-intentionality of consciousness in distinction from cognition which is here proposed by Wojtyła.

26. See preceding note. I take "does not seem to be derived from acts of consciousness" to mean "not strictly caused by," though in some other sense and in their own way, the acts of consciousness take into account the objects of cognition. I take it too that consciousness for the most part does not actually and directly experience the cognitive processes that go into the formation and constitution of the object; hence these processes fall outside the present analysis, though they are open to the more general metaphysical analysis in terms of causality.—In this passage (*AP* 32) the author denies that acts of consciousness as such penetrate the objects, but later (at *AP* 33) he speaks of consciousness as such "penetrating and mirroring," in the sense of a "penetrative illumination" that keeps objects of cognition in the light of the field of consciousness but that does not as such constitute them. Once again, I take it that "penetration" is used here in each passage in two different senses: as "cognitive constitution" in the first passage and as "mirroring or reflecting what is already constituted" in the second. He remarks: "But such penetrative illumination is not tantamount to the active understanding of objects and, subsequently, to the constituting of their meanings" (ibid.).

tio—terms that stand for the properly theoretical activity of the mind. And I suggest that the terms mirroring and enlightening deliberately provide us with echoes of older metaphysical traditions, found particularly in Augustinianism and the medieval *Lichtmetaphysik,* as well as in the Aristotelianism upon which St. Thomas has drawn.

In further description, he tells us that reflecting consciousness penetrates and illuminates "whatever becomes in any way man's cognitive possession" (*AP* 33). One is again put in mind of what traditional philosophy has called "immanence," that interior "light" which belongs to consciousness as such, the proper sphere of its activity by which the mind appropriates its received contents according to its own immaterial mode. And indeed, Wojtyła himself remarks that "consciousness not only reflects but also interiorizes in its own specific manner what it mirrors, thus enclosing or capturing it in the person's ego" (*AP* 34). In mirroring the immanent contents served up by cognitive activity, consciousness becomes "aware," although this "illumination" is not at all the same as cognitive objectification. Here, then, are the beginnings of a phenomenological description of consciousness as spirit, even though the full reality of spirit is not completely accessible to such a description. Nevertheless, it is a description that can be drawn from the experience of our own moral causality as we exercise it in the actions we perform.

In its relation to itself, in its self-immanence, consciousness reflects upon the impact that the cognitive relations and their meanings have on itself; in and through its experience of what is in its field, reflective consciousness shapes its self-understanding. By means of such reflection, consciousness brings about that everchanging, inner quasi-object that comprises the self or personality. But the subject of this state of consciousness is not consciousness itself; it is once again, the human being.[27]

To be sure, cognition cooperates closely with consciousness,

27. "Consciousness does not exist as the 'substantive' subject of the acts of consciousness: it exists neither as an independent factor nor as a[n independent] faculty" (*AP* 34, 37).

which is conditioned by the objects of cognition; in this sense, "the meanings of things . . . are given to consciousness, as it were, from outside as the product of knowledge. . . . Hence the various degrees of knowledge determine the different levels of consciousness" (*AP* 25). Now, the cognition of things is not self-knowledge. Knowledge of the self has as its inner object the ego. "For all the intimacy of its subjective union with the ego, [consciousness itself] does not objectivize the ego or anything else. This function is performed by acts of self-knowledge themselves," which grasp the ego cognitively as an object of self-knowledge. Self-knowledge joins consciousness with cognition and determines the actual limit of consciousness at any given time or in any given situation (*AP* 36). Self-knowledge objectivizes the awareness the human agent has of the self and of one's action (*AP* 37).

These distinctions within the field of consciousness—cognition, self-knowledge, and consciousness as such—arise out of a broader and deeper human potentiality. Now, self-knowledge, knowledge of the self or ego—this means of the concrete ego, this self at this time and in relation to this action—gives rise to a further modification in the field of consciousness, namely, to self-consciousness (*AP* 31–41).

So far, Wojtyła has laid out the intentionality associated with cognitive activities and their grasp of external objects: this is the ordinary sense of "knowing something." He has also set forth the sphere of immanence, which is the mark of consciousness itself. Furthermore, within the immanent field of consciousness, he has set forth the bridge between consciousness as such and an immanent form of reflection, namely, the quasi-objectification of the ego in self-knowledge. It is from this self-knowledge that we form our quasi-objective understanding of ourselves as agents, as well as of ourselves as human beings.

∾

Wojtyła has been considering consciousness as an aspect of the whole human being. He now approaches the very center of consciousness itself (*AP* 41–46). At this point, Wojtyła alerts us again to the phenomenological approach to consciousness, that is, to the experience of consciousness as such in its own interiority. To account for this experience (*doświadczenie*), neither the function of cognition nor that of mirroring is adequate. Cognition and reflection are processes engaged directly or indirectly in objectification; but consciousness in itself is essentially subjective. Only with the experience of its own subjectivity can consciousness experience its actions as its own. To put the matter personally, only in this way can we experience our actions as our own (*AP* 42). Our actions are thereby incorporated into the sphere of our own subjectivity, without in any way disclaiming their objective status and import.

In this very subtle analysis Wojtyła is claiming for realism, and on the basis of experience, the inner reality of the human agent. A realist by intent, Wojtyła has appropriated tools used mostly by idealists, in order to introduce subjectivity into realism. He is concerned to purge these tools of their idealistic distortion in order to free them from the error of asserting consciousness as the absolute subject. At the same time, he is bent upon articulating the interiority of the human reality in a way that is not accessible to metaphysics with its comprehensive consideration of that human reality in terms of a specific kind of being and according to specific modes of existence.

But, if such experience is inaccessible to metaphysics, neither is the true nature of experience disclosed by cognition and reflection. Neither cognitive nor reflective activity actually brings the nature of experience to light; only a distinctive turning back and in to the subject constitutes experience. Wojtyła calls this turn of consciousness upon itself *reflexive*; and he distinguishes reflexivity from reflection or reflectiveness. In reflexive consciousness, man does not merely have knowledge of himself as ego; he experiences himself as subject and identifies that experience with the ego, and precisely with himself as a human being in action: "We then discern clearly that it is one thing to *be* the subject, another to *be cognized* (that is, objectivized) as the subject, and a still different thing to *experience* one's self as the subject of one's own acts and experiences" (*AP* 44). Metaphysics grasps the human reality as subject of being and of action (*suppositum*); cognition grasps the subject intentionally as an "object" from which constitutive acts of knowing arise; but neither metaphysics nor cognition penetrates to the very experience of the exercise of one's own concrete agency. In other words, in its reflexive function, consciousness is not simply a surface epiphenomenon (as materialism would have it); nor does it absorb all of the human reality into its constitutive activity (as idealism would have it). Consciousness in its reflexive function discloses inwardly the reality of the whole human being in the lived experience of its action (*AP* 46).[28]

Now, the whole human being includes all of its constitutive elements—existential, physical, cognitive, and reflective, including the moral norms and the status of the ego in relation to the norms, so that the action is experienced as good or bad, in one or more senses of these terms, and above all in the moral sense. In words reminiscent of the theater of the living word, Wojtyła tells us that this reflexive awareness is at the root of the "remarkable drama of human innerness, the drama of good and evil enacted on the interior stage of the human person by and among his actions." Self-knowledge, then, begins with reflexive self-consciousness and proceeds through the ego toward the external world, including other persons and oneself, and moves back from the outside toward the inner consciousness of one's own subjectivity. This continually developing interplay of inner and outer constitutes my knowledge of myself as both subject and object (*AP* 48–50, 211, 305).

At the very center of our consciousness, then, we experience ourselves reflexively as the source of our actions. We do not experience ourselves simply in the field of conscious thought, but as the source that initiates and executes the actions of our person by drawing upon the fullness of our being. Such reflexive consciousness is not knowledge in any ordinary sense. It is intentional neither in the primary sense of cognition nor even in the secondary reflective sense of relating to that inner quasi-object which is the self as ego. Rather, reflexive consciousness is the experience—or that dimen-

28. See the extended discussion of "reflexivity" (correlated with metaphysical "intransitivity") in Wojtyła's "The Person: Subject and Community," *Review of Metaphysics* 33, no. 2 (Dec. 1979): 273–308, esp. 286.

sion or moment within our experience—in which we sense our own agency.[29]

In refusing to concede that intentionality is the all-pervasive and primary characteristic of consciousness, Wojtyła distinguishes himself from those phenomenologists who insist that the overbearing characteristic of consciousness is that it is through and through object-related and intentional. It is paradoxical that he takes this position in order to defend realism. He argues that a consciousness whose essential trait is intentional would be one that, in constituting its world, would absorb that world into itself as an absolute subject. This idealism, he maintains, falsifies the actual experience we have of consciousness.

It seems to me that such a consciousness would be bound into the web of the world, even as it absorbs that world into its own structures and dynamics. It seems to me, too, that Wojtyła's departure from the prevalent position among phenomenologists—pressed so vigorously by him—provides for the opening to transcendence.[30] Such an opening, first of all, secures our liberty from total immersion in the world of objects. Secondly, it secures that liberty in which—as a theologian, churchman and student of St. John of the Cross—Wojtyła recognizes the opening to grace at the very center of human existence.[31] As a result, the liberty of which

29. Cf. Kant's principle of transcendental apperception: "*Ich bin bewusst.* . . . I am aware that all my representations are mine" (*Kritik der reinen Vernunft* B 138). Of course, just as with Kant's practical principle ("Treat all persons as ends") so frequently quoted approvingly by Wojtyła, the Kantian principle of theoretical subjectivity is also shorn of its critical idealism by Wojtyła. Nonetheless, Wojtyła tells us that Kant contributed to the understanding of self-determination. Cf. also K. Wojtyła, "The Personal Structure of Self-Determination," in *Tommaso d'Aquino nel sou VII centenario* (Rome, 1974), pp. 379–90; also "Participation or Alienation?" *Analecta Husserliana* 6 (1977): 63; and "The Transcendence of the Person in Action and Man's Self-Teleology," *Analecta Husserliana* 9 (1979): 203–12.

30. "Consciousness opens the way to the emergence of the spirituality of the human being and gives us an insight into it. . . . Although it seems that the foundations, or rather the roots of human spirituality lie beyond the direct scope of experience—we only reach them by inference [may we say, by metaphysics, at least in part?]—spirituality itself has its distinctive experiential expression shaping itself through the complete sequence of its manifestations" (*AP* 47). "Spirituality" here, surely, includes "vertical transcendence."

31. Is this not the "fissure" that Adam half-begrudges God in *Radiation of Fatherhood*?

Wojtyła speaks is different from that existentialist liberty that falls back defiantly upon human resources alone.[32]

We realize the experience of liberty, however, only on the basis of the experience of our own efficacy (*sprawczość*), i.e., the experience that we are capable of self-possession and self-governance through our self-determination (*AP* 99–100, 105ff.).[33] It is in ourselves that the drama of our liberty is played out, and it is played through what we do.[34] The human person is more than his or her liberty; but it is in action that the whole person is gathered into the task of responsible freedom. If we are to possess ourselves and to govern ourselves through our liberty, then we are faced with the task of integration—not only of coordinating the various strands of our consciousness, but of integrating into our actions our whole human being, body and soul, *physis* and *psychē* (*AP* 189ff.).

∽

Such integration is indeed a task. For if we are not *Actus Purus* as God is, neither are we even *actio pura,* pure action through and through. As Wojtyła turns to examine the task of personal integration to which we are called, he begins with a capital distinction between activity and passivity, between what we do and what merely happens to us. The difference is not only conceptual, it is

32. At this point I pass over the analysis of "The Element of Consciousness and the Emotive Element in Man," and, in particular, of the manner in which the emotionalization of consciousness affects the twofold function of consciousness, viz., mirroring and reflexivity (*AP* 50–56). It is just this emotive element that plays an indispensable role in his dramas of the inner living word. I also pass over an important discussion of subjectivity and subjectivism (*AP* 56–59).

33. The first edition of the English text has been heavily edited in this section (especially, for example, *AP* 72–75, 93–99, 118–19), and can even prove treacherous to the unwary reader. Latin technical terms have been left out or paraphrased, and paragraph-long references to medieval thought have been omitted. At *AP* 108 (in what may have simply been a misprint) "inter-" (between) should read "intra-" (within, inner), an important emendation for Wojtyła's thought. The English (at *AP* 113) reads "objectification," whereas it has been pointed out to me that the first Polish edition (at 118) reads "subjectification"; this seems to me to be the proper reading.

34. In "The Intentional Act and the Human Act," p. 275, Wojtyła writes of the " '*drama of the will.*' The expression '*drama*' is to be taken here literally as a dynamism proper to the human will . . . a battle of motives, *felt very definitely as an interior struggle.*" This recalls his remarks about the "realism" of the theater, and also (in *The Jeweler's Shop*) about the struggle to realize love as "the constant challenge thrown to us by God."

a fact of our experience.[35] We experience ourselves as acting or as being acted upon (*AP* 61, 65ff., 71ff., 87).[36]

On the one hand, we do things freely and deliberately, and these are properly human actions (*actus humanus*). On the other hand, things also simply happen to us. Among these latter happenings are dynamisms that lie wholly or partly outside our control; they include even those dynamisms that may be performed by us, but not in the precisely human sense: they are merely *actus hominis*. These latter dynamisms, while dynamic in their own terms, "depend on a certain passiveness in man" and are not dynamic in the same sense that the properly human acts are. Indeed, they pursue ends that, taken in themselves, may differ from those that may be chosen by our liberty (*AP* 97–98).

The author distinguishes two general kinds of dynamism that belong more or less to the domain of what happens to us, as distinct from what we do. There are, first of all, the *somato–vegetative* dynamisms, such as the circulation of the blood, digestion, and the like. These seldom enter into conscious experience, and then only indirectly (*AP* 88–92). Their analysis is best left to the special sciences, and in a more fundamental sense to metaphysics and its account of human nature as *suppositum*. And yet, since it is the whole human being who acts, these dynamisms must be brought from the status of mere conditions external to one's acting to become as far as possible ingredients within one's agency.[37]

35. The distinction is between "man-acts" and "something-happens-in-man," and the further distinction is drawn between "in" (*w*) and "with-man" (*z*). The latter expresses what happens to man from the outside, while the former most properly expresses the concept of "subjectiveness" (*AP* 62–63). Wojtyła wonders whether this is not the "most primitive" experiential distinction, and he likens it to Aristotle's distinction of *poiein-paschein* or *pathein* (*Metaphysics* 1046a19–22), though the latter is interpreted metaphysically (*AP* 306, n. 27).

36. At this point the analysis takes up such themes as the apparent opposition of nature and person, and the need to integrate nature (along with the natural elements of the human being) into the person (*AP* 78–80). There is also a discussion of the metaphysical as distinct from the phenomenological articulation of existence and *suppositum* (though the word is paraphrased variously in the first English edition); and a discussion of the relation of potentiality and act in the realization of the person.

37. See chapter 5, "Integration and the Soma" (*AP* 189–218). Wojtyła later

The *psycho-emotive* dynamisms, on the other hand, offer more to consciousness. They are the dynamisms of perception and imagining, sensation, feeling and emotion. They not only enter into conscious experience, but they make up a good part of its content.[38] Feelings and emotions play a portentous role within the self-determination of the acting person (*AP* 91–92, 227–31). Single experiences with emotional content may, upon recurrence, become regular states, and these may come to be formed into more permanent attitudes, which in turn give tone to our whole experience as persons (*AP* 213ff., 251ff. with reference to skills). The task of integration, then, includes that of incorporating the psycho-emotive dynamisms into the values of one's personal project and character.

Despite the emphasis upon the reflexivity by which we are conscious of our own agency, we must not forget that consciousness is only an aspect of the whole human being, and by no means its sole dynamic source. We have already remarked that the entire complex that makes up the human being is constituted in large part by dynamisms that are by no means identical with the motivations of consciousness. We are also constituted in part by the somato-vegetative dynamisms with their own rhythms, which remain for the most part inaccessible to consciousness; and by the psycho-emotive dynamisms that feed much of our conscious life without being identical with the intellectual facets of consciousness itself.

Among the psycho-emotive dynamisms, those of particular importance are the subconscious dynamisms that, more forcefully than the others, indicate the complex depth at which the human being moves and is moved (*AP* 92–95).[39] On the negative side,

---

develops a thoroughgoing "theology of the body"; in the next chapter, he points out that we experience the body primarily through feeling (*AP* 228).

38. The discussion in chapter 6, "Personal Integration and the Psyche" (*AP* 220–58), derives in part from the author's interest in Scheler and the work of certain psychologists. A. Półtawski, "Personal Integration and the Psyche," *Analecta Husserliana* 7 (1978): 115–50, compares Wojtyła's analysis with that of Henri Ey. See also the admirable resumé of *AP* at pp. 116–25.

39. See A. Półtawski, ibid., particularly pp. 123–25.

and according to psychoanalysis, the subconscious censors the emotive dynamisms. Wojtyła is not quite satisfied with this emphasis, however. He concedes that, along with the other dynamisms, the subconscious pursues its own ends; but he asks whether we should not also look upon this half-secret dynamism as contributing to the development of the whole human being. In his discussion of drives and reflexes,[40] Wojtyła is at pains to insist that, while they are closely related to the somatic needs of the body, the drives and reflexes also include psycho-emotive elements; more than that, they include the deep stirrings within the whole human being in which the subconscious plays its part as well (*AP* 92–95, 215–19).

In relation to consciousness, the subconscious opens up what Wojtyła calls an inner space below the level of experience: a dimension of "sub-experience." Its objects are often enough suppressed; but, on the other hand, they may be released into consciousness. In this way the subconscious is sometimes a defense mechanism, but at other times it is a bridge that provides for and mediates the unity of the complex mechanisms that make up the whole human being. Indeed, in the strivings of the subconscious toward expression, Wojtyła finds an indication of the rich potentiality and unity of the human subject, "the inner continuity and cohesion of the subject," which comprises the "internal history" possessed by each individual. Wojtyła concludes:

There is something highly significant in the constant drive [on the part of the subconscious] toward the light of consciousness, in the constant urge emanating from the subconscious to attain the level of consciousness and to be consciously experienced . . . [for] consciousness is the sphere where man most appropriately fulfills himself. (*AP* 95)

Could we perhaps say that, in terms of metaphysics, this drive for light is the drive to realize the *rationale* in the animal rationale;

40. In the first English edition the term for "drive" in the Polish has been rendered throughout as "instinct," although the author explicitly distinguishes the two terms (*AP* 238). At *AP* 228 "stimuli" in the first English edition is rendered by the corrected version as "response," and both "impulse" and "reflection" as "reflex."

and that, in terms of phenomenology, this drive is the experience (and often the struggle) to realize the potentiality for meaning that is inherent in the human person? At any rate, Wojtyła suggests that one of the chief tasks of morality and of education is to release into consciousness those genuinely human moments that may be held captive in the subconscious. Here speaks the experience of the poet and dramatist.

༄

Nevertheless, at the center of the personal project of each human being is the individual's conscious agency (*AP* 156). Because his action arises out of his free self-determination, in his acting the individual transcends himself as *suppositum*,[41] even as he transcends his subconscious and the complex of dynamisms operating within him (*AP* 155–56).

It is significant here that the author uses a specific Polish word to designate each person's control over his or her properly human acts. He does not use the general term for power (*moc*). Instead, he uses the term for executive power (*władza*), which is equivalent to the Latin *actus humanus* and means "the voluntary rational exercise of power" (*AP* 122).[42] The personal project, then, is carried out through self-determining actions grounded in self-possession and self-governance (*AP* 105ff., 151, 161–62, 173).

The action is filled, however, only through the agent's appropriation of and subordination of his action to the goods or good that alone can realize the fullness of the concrete possibilities of each human person. Feelings in themselves do not determine values or our knowledge of them—the reference is to the author's ongoing critique of Scheler—though they frequently accompany our relation to them: "The fusion of sensitivity with truthfulness is

41. Here the first English edition is without the qualification "in the sense of traditional metaphysics" (*AP* 153); nor does the Latin term *transcendentalia* appear (*AP* 155–57).

42. In "The Intentional Act and the Human Act, Act and Experience," p. 270, speaking of the general sense of the term "human act," Wojtyła remarks: "As such it does not, like the intentional act, stop at one rational element—on the contrary it represents the complete personality, that is, the complete man. . . ." For the remainder of this important text, see chap. 2, note 23, above.

the necessary condition of the experience of values" (*AP* 233). And truthfulness transcends the sensory level of feelings.

On the other hand, neither are values determined through our choice. On the contrary, values are "normogenic"; they generate norms for the acting person (*AP* 311, n. 52). These norms are the directives of being, of reality; so that here again, we touch upon the borders of metaphysics:

> There is no question but that the conception of man as person—though it is accessible in the original intuition within the frame of phenomeno-logical insight—has to be completed and supplemented by the metaphys-ical analysis of the human being. Thus while the experience of the personal unity of man shows us his complex nature, the attempt at a deepened understanding of this complexity allows us in turn to interpret the human composite (*compositum humanum*) as the one and ontically unique per-son. (*AP* 186)[43]

In this acknowledgment of the role of metaphysics, we also rec-ognize the objective order of goods as part of the real order of beings. Even prior to the consideration of the moral quality of ac-tion, action itself is not merely subjective. Its subjective efficacy does indeed come from the power of self-determination exercised by the agent, but its objective efficacy arises out of an objective order that is also manifested in and through that action (*AP* 68, 109).[44]

Indeed, pure subjectiveness—we might say, the distinctive mode of human passivity—belongs, not to action (to "man-acts"), but to the dimension of what merely happens to man (*AP* 80, 120). Values are not subjective and are not constituted by subjectiveness.

43. The first English edition reads "human nature" instead of "the human com-posite (*compositum humanum*)."

44. After remarking that ordinary intentionality, including the intentionality of willing, "does not properly appertain to self-determination," Wojtyła adds: "For in self-determination we do not turn to the ego as the object [i.e., we do not will the ego], we only impart actuality to the, so to speak, ready-made objectiveness [the content of the shape or image] of the ego which is contained in the intraper-sonal relation of self-governance and self-possession. This imparting of actuality is of fundamental significance in morality, that specific dimension of the human, per-sonal existence which is simultaneously both subjective and objective. It is there that the whole reality of morals, of moral values, has its roots" (*AP* 109).

Indeed, if I do not overstate the author's realism on this point, while all the subjective elements that partially constitute the human person may come into play in action, values do not differ in reality from goods; they are those same goods insofar as they offer to the person the genuine possibility of becoming more effectively human. It is here that the metaphysics of the good joins the phenomenology of value within the human and personal act.

Now, this more effective and efficacious humanness is gained through the interplay of integration and transcendence: "Integration complements the transcendence of the person, which is realized through self-determination and efficacy" (*AP* 225). Neither integration nor transcendence can proceed without each other, both call for the orchestration of our freedom. It is an orchestration whose melody is the truth that is normative for practical life (*AP* 158–65). The capacity to respond to values—in a word, "truthfulness"—and the experienced fact of responsibility that flows from that capacity presuppose the specific "relation to truth in which obligation is rooted as the normative power of truth" (*AP* 170). It is here that conscience in its truthfulness is the medium through which truth speaks to the human person and agent in terms of its normative power and in the light of apprehended values.

Freedom, then, is not an indiscriminate lack of direction, an arbitrary impulse. "Freedom is expressed by efficacy, and efficacy leads to responsibility" (*AP* 180).[45] It is important to stress the term efficacy, for in it lies the truly creative potential of human action. Through our human acts (*actus humanus*) we effect ourselves and other persons and things; and in this efficacy lies the root of our responsibility. Freedom is experienced in the form, "I could but I need not" (*AP* 120);[46] and in its fullness in the form of

45. "The one who acts *is* the person and asserts himself as 'somebody' [and not just 'something'] . . . He shows himself as having the special ability and power of self-governance which allows him to have the experience of himself as a free being" (*AP* 180).
46. The first English edition reads: "I may . . .," which bears a quite different meaning.

the relation of "obligation-responsibility," that is, in the form, "I should" (*AP* 170).[47] And so, Kant's insight is by no means simply swept aside.

On the subjective side, human freedom is rooted in the very structure of the human person, and the subjective measure of our freedom is the degree to which we have succeeded in integrating the complex strands of our consciousness and the various dynamisms within our whole being as concrete persons. In the degree to which someone has achieved such integration, he or she has realized the inherent and unique potentiality of his or her concrete personhood.

On the objective side—and this may surprise those who associate the term exclusively with the subjective—there is conscience. Conscience (*sumienie*) is the capacity in us to recognize the values and disvalues among the range of possible actions facing each of us (*AP* 158–65, 173).[48] Of course, conscience is subjective inasmuch as it seizes upon the norm as it functions within the context of a particular person; but it opens the person out onto the genuine, objective good of that person and opens the person to that which is common and universal, that is to say, to what is human, and beyond that even to what is ontological in that good. In this sense, conscience is a kind of knowing that is not an ordinary knowing; it is rather a sense of truthfulness that is not theoretical or cognitive, but that is rooted instead in our existential embodiment and that is oriented toward the individual's practical decisions and actions.

Nor is conscience merely a passive acknowledgement of norms, as though they apply externally and by compulsion. Conscience is

47. "The Intentional Act and the Human Act," pp. 275–76, stresses the link between conscience and obligation.

48. "As manifested in man's conscience, the capacity to surrender to truth shows how deeply the relation to truth is rooted in the potentiality of the personal being of man. It is this capacity, with its persuasive and prompting power, that we have in mind when we speak of the 'rational nature' of man, or when we attribute to his mind the ability to know moral truth and to distinguish it from moral falsehood" (*AP* 158).

creative, not in the sense that it departs arbitrarily from truth and from the capacity for truthfulness, but because

the conscience plays a creative role in what concerns the truthfulness of norms, that is to say, of those principles of acting and behavior which form the objective core of morality or law. Its creativity goes beyond simple recognition of the norm or injunction that generates the sense of obligation resulting in passive obedience. The experience of rightness is preceded and integrated by the experience of truthfulness which inheres in the acceptance of a norm that relies upon the strength of the subjective conviction. (*AP* 165)

Conscience is that peculiar kind of knowing that "knows" the norm insofar as it applies concretely to this or that person in terms of the values at stake in their relation to the person (*AP* 156–62).

So, too, if we understand by the will the faculty of choice, there is a liberty in each of us that is more than the freedom of the will: "The elementary manifestation of free will simultaneously brings to light the person's exclusive power to control the will [through auto-determination]. . . . It is because of the person's exclusive power over the will that *will is the person's power to be free*" (*AP* 122ff). And, while he respects the traditional discussion of freedom in terms of the will, Wojtyła asks rhetorically: "Does not the will as a power inhere in the person, in that self-determination whereby the person manifests his appropriate structure? It is for this reason that to reduce the content of volition to will seen solely as a power, may to some extent impoverish the reality contained in action" (*AP* 322–23). It is here that a metaphysics of being needs to be supplemented and interiorized by a phenomenology of inner experience, whose dramatic equivalent is a theater of the inner word.

This freedom of action is nothing other than the liberty of the person. For the human person is not determined by the will, but conversely the human person freely determines the will in his or her active self-determination. This is, surely, an old insight given new life, namely, the insight that it is neither the intellect that knows nor the will that decides, but it is the human being as acting person who recognizes, initiates, and determines. To act with efficacy is to integrate the rich complexity of the embodied human agent in a way that transforms him or her. And to do this, the acting person needs both integration and transcendence, which are inseparable in the fulfillment of properly human action.

Action, then, redounds upon the whole person, so that self-determination is also self-formation and self-development. Herein lies the reason why an action is not merely a quality or property of a person, and why it leaves the whole person either better or worse. Only in transcendence do we go beyond ourselves toward the promise of each one's unique humanity.[49] Part of our fulfillment consists in a horizontal transcendence, that is, in our going out to the things around us, in coming to know them, in interacting with them and being affected by them. But such horizontal transcendence is only a condition of our fulfillment: it is not its key.

∾

The threshold that we must cross is upwards; it lies beyond us. We are called, therefore, to vertical transcendence, that very transcendence which, in *The Jeweler's Shop*, is said to cut through every married love—and which is at the source of every love. We are called to a vertical transcendence, in the sense that we are called to progress toward the highest realization of values. In this way, genuine change takes place in us, as we return to ourselves, once we have surrendered the self that we presently are to the self that we might become. It is this self-surrender that Adam finds so hard to accomplish in *Radiation of Fatherhood*.

The progress toward vertical transcendence is not a solitary journey, however. For the actions that transform a person are for the most part taken together with others. And so, in the final chapter, the author takes up the topic of interpersonal relations and of participation in community with others for the benefit of the whole (*AP* 262ff., 322ff.).[50] This supplement helps to correct any impres-

49. In *Radiation of Fatherhood* (part 1, scene 2 [*CP*, p. 338]), Adam recognizes in each individual an unrealized substance of humanity.
50. The author published "Person: Subject and Community" as an addendum

sion that his insistence upon the responsibility of each person is an advocacy of individualism. We have already seen the sense of community dramatized; indeed, Wojtyła understands modern individualism to spring from the same defects as modern collectivism. Neither of them can establish a genuine community, which can be achieved only by human beings acting as the persons they in fact are and might become (AP 271–76).

The emphasis upon the person is meant to underline the truth that human relationships are possible only insofar as personal reality is present and operative in the relationships. Nor is this a truism, given the forces of de-personalization that are all too common in modern times. The emphasis upon unique persons carries forward the existential demand that human relationships must be concrete if they are to be actual. And so, his interest in participation in this study is not in a merely general sense of togetherness, nor even in social and political forms of togetherness, but in "the genuinely personalistic structure of human existence in a community, that is, in every community that man belongs to" (AP 282, 338).

Wojtyła's earlier interest in St. Augustine's notion of participation (LV 155) has been deepened through his own analysis of personal action. Indeed, his emphasis throughout the study has not even been directly on the ethical rightness of human actions, but on their value as fulfilling the person; that is to say, on their authentically personalistic value. The focus is upon "the performance of the action and the fulfillment [of the person] in the action" (AP 270). We might add here that Wojtyła's focus is upon action insofar as it transforms the person for better or for worse. While in no way downplaying the indispensable and perfective role of ethics, Wojtyła tells us that his attention in The Acting Person has been directed to the anthropological foundations of action and to the personal value "that belongs to the performance itself of the action, to its personal subjectiveness—an 'inner' norm concerned

to chap. 7 of AP in Review of Metaphysics 33, no. 2 (Dec. 1979): 273–308. In "Participation or Alienation?" Analecta Husserliana 6 (1977): 64, the author identifies the potential neighbor with every (human) other.

with safeguarding the self-determination of the person; it also safeguards his efficacy as well as his transcendence and integration in the action" (*AP* 328). The study is offered, then, as a contribution to philosophical anthropology in the Christian and Catholic tradition. By participation, Wojtyła means to signal actions performed by a person together with other persons in such a way that the integration and transcendence appropriate to each person is realized through such actions. The notion of participation is, then, deliberately value laden.

In a touching extension of the meaning of the term and reality of the neighbor, Wojtyła argues that it is not enough to be a member of one or more communities; we are also called upon to be neighbors. Now, assuredly, a neighbor is someone close to us, near not distant; but Wojtyła is not satisfied with this etymological meaning. To be related to another as to a neighbor is to be related to that individual in his or her very being precisely as a concrete human being. But this, he concludes, is nothing other than the commandment of love, the vocation to juxtapose my neighbor with myself (*AP* 292–99, 348–55). Our call to personal transcendence is a call to act with others in realizing the mutual dignity of being persons.

Wojtyła's intense study of human action has been undertaken to disclose the ontological worth of the human person, a dignity that lies prior to and provides the ground for the axiological value of personal action (*AP* 264, 320). The personalistic value of human action is constituted by the following factors: (1) performance by the person, (2) in a manner appropriate to his or her nature as human, and so (3) according to self-determination through the capacity for reflection, reflexivity, practical reason, and the decisive will. In authentic action the person realizes (4) the transcendence uniquely and properly his or hers, while at the same time (5) advancing the integration of both *soma* and *psyche,* (6) in an efficacious way that satisfies the requirements of both the subjective and the objective sides of that being which in its entirety is at once human and personal.

Questions remain ("Postscript," *AP* 299–300, 355–57); but

the central question, "Why be moral?" has received a long, convoluted, and in many respects, a fresh answer. The study has sought to manifest the existential structure of concrete human action in such a way that the act of putting the question is answered by the very character of action itself. Because action draws upon the whole person as agent, it affects the whole person; and because ethical action engages the good of the person through personalistic values, it cannot leave the person indifferent to his or her action. It transforms the person, for better or for worse.

The structure of the human person, however, is such that the individual human being is called to integrate his or her complex dynamisms and to redeem the promise of what is both a received human nature and a unique personal project. The realization of the value of one's person comes through actions that are responsible, that are self-determined and yet responsive to the enlarged sense of reality in which both the subjective and objective sides of human existence are in play. The inwardness of the person has been shown by a phenomenological realism; and the more general features of the human condition have been illuminated by a metaphysics of existential act that gives its account in terms of concrete agency. The integral analysis discloses the human person as called to act in communion with others in the realization of his or her possibilities; beyond that, we are called to act in accordance with a reality that transcends us on all sides. In that communion and transcendence we are awakened to new possibilities that entirely transcend the limits of human action. Those possibilities are disclosed in the very revelation of our beginnings; and to that revelation we now turn.

CHAPTER IV

From Peter's Chair
A Christian Anthropology

With the turn from Karol Wojtyła the philosopher to John Paul II the Pope, key ideas and emphases, salient insights and directions of thought continue to be expressed in his teaching, even as some of the earliest themes were already dramatically declaimed in his theater of the living word. The most prominent of these arch-ideas is the insistence that mankind—men and women—must return to their transcendent Source, if they are to find the fulfilment of their destiny and their hopes. You will recall Adam's remark to Anna in *The Jeweler's Shop*, that on the other side of all human loves there is Love; and again, in *Radiation of Fatherhood*, you will recall the image of the stream from which the grace of healing baptism flows as from its Source. And in *Our God's Brother*, Adam the painter struggles to move beyond the visual images of his art towards the nonpictorial image buried in his soul, which constitutes the reality, the truth, and the value of his own humanity. Finally, in *The Acting Person* Wojtyła's denial of intentionality as definitive of the essential nature and function of consciousness discloses the basis on which consciousness breaks free into its self-transcending movement. Wojtyła insists upon this, because it is in the Source more clearly than anywhere else that the original intent of the Creator and the original orientation of the human creature is most clearly revealed. For there, in the Source, is revealed in the bright mystery of creation, the mystery of the "radiation of Fatherhood."

In order to round out this sketch of the anthropology of Karol Wojtyła/John Paul II, then, I have chosen to illustrate the original human project as the pope has addressed the topic in theological terms in the first of his "Wednesday Talks," the *Discorsi* he held in the Pope Paul VI Aula. The thousands who attended had, I suppose, come for the most part simply to see the new pope, who had already become something of a remarkable public figure. What they made of the talks I do not know, but I suspect that the pontiff could have danced a jig or performed tricks to their satisfaction since they had come to see him. Others with more erudition, who had come to listen, professed themselves at a difficult loss at times to follow the line of discourse. Indeed, it is no doubt true that the *Talks* would tax the ability of an audience hearing these ideas for the first time and in such a setting, for the talks make little concession to their hearers. They bring to my mind a small puzzle that scholars of St. Augustine would surely solve for me: to what sort of an audience did the African saint address his magnificent sermons? Well, in a somewhat analogous fashion, one finds in the *Talks* the result of years of prolonged meditation upon the deepest aspects of the Christian faith. And so, they are meant to be re-read—and reread for insights that are at once fresh and profound. This is especially true of the first series, which has appeared in English under the title *Original Unity of Man and Woman*; lectures in the first series were given from September 5, 1979, to April 2, 1980.[1] The first talks concentrate upon the biblical texts of Genesis, precisely the opening four chapters, and for the most part upon the first two.

As Pope John Paul II turns to consider the significance of the texts of Genesis 1 and 2, he does not speak primarily as a Scripture scholar (though he is well informed regarding that scholarship and finds it helpful at a number of points); he speaks rather as theologian and philosopher, even more as a person of religious faith, and in the first place as mandated teacher.

Before turning to the ancient biblical texts themselves, he first

1. The subtitle is *Catechesis on the Book of Genesis* (Daughters of St. Paul: Boston, 1980), from the translation published in the English edition of *Osservatore Romano*. Subsequent volumes in the same series are *Blessed Are the Pure of Heart: Catechesis on the Sermon on the Mount and Writings of St. Paul* (April 16, 1980–May 6, 1981) and *Reflections on Humanae Vitae: Conjugal Morality and Spirituality* (July 11–November 28, 1984).

turns to Christ. In particular, he considers the saying of Christ in answer to the Pharisees, who put forward Moses' certificate of divorce against the indissolubility of marriage. To this Christ replied (Matt. 19:3ff., Cf., Mark 10:2ff.) that Moses had permitted divorce because of the hardness of their hearts; and then Christ added: "But in the beginning it was not so."[2] From this reply on the part of Christ, John Paul looks back with the authoritative light of Christ to the beginning, to the moment of creation, before sin came into the world. In so doing, he looks back toward the Source, in order to see what God intended regarding this profound human relationship of marriage, and what God had in mind more generally concerning the nature and destiny of man.[3]

2. Here are the relevant passages from the New Testament (Matt. 19:3–6 [*RSV*]): "And Pharisees came up to him and tested him by asking: 'Is it lawful to divorce one's wife for any cause?' He answered, "Have you not read that the Creator from the beginning made them male and female [*arsen kai thēlu*]? [Gen. 1:27; 5:2]. And he said: For this reason a man must leave father and mother, and be joined to his wife and the two shall become one? [Gen. 2:24: *esontai hai duo eis sarka mian*: the two become one flesh, one body]. So, they are no longer two, but one [body]. What therefore God has joined together, let no man put asunder."— It is, then, with his own authority and on the basis of Gen. 2:24 that Christ restores the indissolubility of marriage and pronounces remarriage of divorced persons adultery. And Matt. 19:8 (*Jerusalem/RSV*): "He [i.e. Christ] said to them [the Pharisees]: "It [viz., the reason why Moses gave a bill of divorce, *biblion apostasiou*] was because you were so unteachable [*sklērokardían*: your hardness of heart (*RSV*)] that Moses allowed [*epetrepsen*] you to divorce [*apolūsai*] your wives; but from the beginning it was not so [*ap archēs de ou gōgonen houtōs*]." Also Mark 10:5–9 (*Jerusalem*): Then Jesus said to them, "It was because you were unteachable [obdurate] that he [i.e., Moses] wrote this commandment [*entolēn*] for you. But from the beginning of creation [*apo de archēs ktiseōs*] he [i.e., God] made them male and female [Gen. 1:27]. This is why a man must leave father and mother, and the two become one body [Gen. 2:24]. They are no longer two, therefore, but one body [*mia sarx*]. So, then, what God has united, man must not divide." Christ has framed his teaching on the basis of the combined texts of Genesis 1 and 2 taken together; but He has considerably deepened the intimacy of the union. (Cf. Jesus' similar joining of the two great commandments: to love God [Deut. 6:5]) and one's neighbor [Lev. 19:18].) Christ follows with the warning, "The man who divorces his wife—I am not speaking of fornication [*porneia*]—and marries [*gamēsē*] another, is guilty of adultery [*moichatai*]" (Matt. 19:9). And (back in the house, to the disciples who questioned him further) he said again (Mark 10:11–12): "The man who divorces his wife and marries another is guilty of adultery towards her. And if a woman divorces her husband and marries another, she is guilty of adultery too."

3. *Original Unity of Man and Woman*, Sept. 5, 1979, sect. 2, p. 16; I will refer to these talks within the text in the following manner: (*OU* S/5/79, 2; 16).

According to biblical scholars, there are two accounts of the creation of man at the beginning of the book of Genesis (*OU* S/5/79, 3; 17). The first account occurs in chapter one, but scholars deem it to be chronologically later. It is thought to have been authored (speaking of the human element in its composition) or edited by the priests, and so it is called the Priestly account. This account situates the creation of man within the cosmic account of the creation of the world in seven days, man being created on the sixth day (Gen. 1:26–29). The second account (in the second and third chapters of Genesis) is thought to be chronologically earlier. It is linked with the story of original innocence and transgression. Because it uses the name Yahweh to refer to God, it is known as the Yahwist account (Gen. 2:5⊥25, and the later events in Gen. 3) (*OU* S/12/79, 1–2; 21). What is especially illuminating according to John Paul II is that, on being asked about a most important and fundamental human relationship, namely, that of marriage and divorce, Christ—speaking with authority—took his questioners back to the beginning, back to the texts that reveal our origins.

The two accounts complement each other, each shedding somewhat different light upon our mysterious origin. It seems to me, too, that the pope—as much poet and dramatist as he is theologian and philosopher—is attracted to the older and as he calls it, the more primitive, Yahwist account, precisely because of its strongly anthropological, even anthropomorphic, character (*OU* S/12/79, 2; 21f.). Nevertheless, he observes that the Priestly account bears within it a more mature reflection upon the human condition, "both as regards the image of God, and as regards the formulation of the essential truths about man" (*OU* S/12/79, 2; 22).

The Priestly account is many-faceted: it is cosmological, anthropological, ethical, theological, and metaphysical. It speaks of man as part of the visible world, hence it is cosmological (Gen. 1:1–27) (*OU* S/12/79, 3; 22). At the same time, it also sets man over the earth as its steward (Gen. 1:28), and so it has anthropological and ethical implications. Stewardship is given to man, however, because man is made in the image and likeness of God (Gen. 1:27); and so the Priestly account is above all theological,

since it defines man in terms of his relationship to God (*OU* S/12/
79, 3–4; 22–23). But the definition is loaded with metaphysical
content as well, since it speaks of man in his concrete existence or
being, man in the very creation by which he comes to be. It is
indeed a rich account.

John Paul points up certain aspects and implications for us today as we read this ancient text. The more reflective Priestly account gives the theological and metaphysical definition of man. It
is theological, as he has said, because it defines us in terms of our
fundamental and originating relationship to God—the relation
of image and likeness; and it is metaphysical, because "man is defined there, first of all, in the dimensions of being and existence
("*Esse*")." And John Paul underscores the metaphysical element
by adding, "He is defined in a way that is more metaphysical than
physical" (*OU* S/12/79, 5; 24). No doubt, the pope's profession
as a philosopher leads him to find considerable significance in this
metaphysical dimension of the text; but he is not alone. Indeed, he
remarks that, along with the famous text of Exodus 3:14 in which
God gives his name as I AM, no other text has provided so much
inspiration and suggestion for metaphysics. For we find recounted
in this text, not only the very act of creation itself, but the absolutely basic distinction between the eternal and necessary being of
God and the radically contingent being of creatures (*OU* S/12/79,
5; 24).

This is not, of course, a metaphysics indifferent to the good; for
it recognizes what John Paul here calls "the aspect of value." We
have already seen much of this term "value," which has a technical
meaning in the philosophical tradition with which he is in some
way associated and to which he has given his own stamp. Along
with the whole of creation, man is not only declared to be good,
however, but is pointed toward a special form of goodness: "[For]
it can be said only of him that a gift was conferred on him: the
visible world was created 'for him.'"[4] This is the first visible fruit

4. The text continues: "The biblical account of creation offers us sufficient rea-

of that dignity of the human person that arises from having been made in the image and likeness of God. Such created dignity is the theological equivalent of the principle so much admired and so often repeated by the philosopher Wojtyła in the words of another philosopher, Immanuel Kant: each person possesses that value by virtue of which he or she is never to be treated merely as a means but always as an end. And it is by virtue of this unique and inherent value that man takes from the hand of God his stewardship of the earth and the procreation of other human beings—and therewith receives the human fatherhood that Adam resisted so much in *Radiation of Fatherhood.*

The text, then, joins being with good, even as their convertibility has been argued again and again by Karol Wojtyła in the *Lublin Lectures.* Moreover, in the *Wednesday Talks,* too, John Paul confirms this interpenetration of existence and value by once again using the scholastic formula: *ens et bonum convertuntur,* where there is being *there* is value, and where there is good, *there too* is being (*OU* S/12/79, 5; 25).

John Paul now draws attention to two disclosures that highlight the distinctive nature of humanity. First, man's creation is announced with a certain fanfare that is absent from the creation of other creatures. It is as though God had stopped to deliberate before undertaking the risk of creating this being who is to be like him in a way that no other creature is: "Let us make man in our own image, in the likeness of ourselves" (Gen. 1:26). You will remember in *Radiation of Fatherhood* the words of querulous Adam, who complained that God had "inflicted" the divine like-

---

sons to understand and interpret in this way: creation is a gift, because there appears in it man who, as the 'image of God,' is capable of understanding the very meaning of gift in the call from nothingness to existence. And he is capable of answering the Creator with the language of this understanding. Interpreting the narrative of creation with this language, it can be deduced from it that creation constitutes the fundamental and original gift: man appears in creation as the one who received the world as a gift, and vice versa it can also be said that the world received man as a gift" (*OU* J/2/80, 4; 104). I have treated the topic in the forty-sixth Aquinas Lecture: *The Gift: Creation* (Milwaukee: Marquette University Press, 1982).

ness upon him—and presumably without consultation! Nor did God consult Adam in regard to the second important development; for the text stresses that, within mankind, God created man different in gender: "male and female He created them" (Gen. 1:27). About that momentous divine decision John Paul has much to say in what follows.

We have already underscored the cosmological character of this later, Priestly account in which man is called upon to multiply and to master the created world.[5] But this call to stewardship is not based primarily upon man's physical makeup or upon the characteristics that he shares with the rest of the visible world; in fact, the biblical text does not mention this general similarity (*OU S/ 12/79*, 3; 22). The call to stewardship is based instead upon man's likeness to God, that is, upon a theological relationship. Later ages have understood this to be a relation centered in God and the human spirit, hence, a spiritual relationship. And so we may infer that the relationship is not one of sheer power and domination, nor even of technological exploitation determined by human will alone; the task given to man by God is a conditional superintendence and use of nature in accordance with the original intention of God. Moreover, in the making of the heavens and the earth, God has already declared the prehuman creation to be good without anticipatory reference to man; and so, it is safe to assume that earth and sky and all living things possess an inherent dignity and value of their own and that their value cannot be overridden by arbitrary human design, even though other creatures do not possess the distinctive value conferred upon man by the image-relationship. In short: mankind is called to stewardship and not to absolute sovereignty.

Now, to be sure, such a teaching is not peculiar to John Paul II. It has been the constant understanding of the Church since the

5. The two Hebrew accounts of this stewardship suggest slightly nuanced differences. The Priestly account reads: "fill the earth, and subdue it [*kābaš*: to tread down, subjugate], and rule over it [*rādâ*: to tread down, have dominion]"; whereas the comparable words in the Yahwist account read: "Yahweh God took the man and put him in the garden of Eden, to work it [*'ābad*: to serve, till, enslave] and to keep it [*šāmar*: to hedge about, protect, guard]."

earliest times, but John Paul sometimes reinforces this element of conditionality in man's dealings with other creatures in new ways. It seems to me that to John Paul II's mind the modern practical tendency to obscure or forget the conditional nature of our stewardship is the direct outcome of the modern theoretical tendency to treat human consciousness as an absolute.[6] The limited character of our superintendence of nature is a lesson that we have tended to forget, especially since the seventeenth century, when excitement over the discovery of the empirical patterns of nature promoted technology and the rush toward the possession of material goods. Indeed, it is only recently, with the problems of overdevelopment,[7] overconsumption, pollution, and other threats to the environment, that the conditional character of man's stewardship has begun once again to be recognized more widely. In any event, the constant teaching of the Church on the moderate use of goods—private property for common use—is surely based in part upon a careful and prayerful reading of the ancient wisdom of this biblical text.[8] This conditional oversight, this stewardship, has great importance for the social teaching of the Church, articulated especially by the great social encyclicals of the popes since Leo XIII and emphasized by the present pontiff in three encyclicals during the past ten years.[9]

Turning to the second, older account, the Yahwist account of

6. See the discussion of the modern absolutization of human consciousness in the final chapter.

7. *Redemptoris Missio* IV, sec. 59, speaks of the north as "prone to a moral and spiritual poverty caused by 'overdevelopment'." This recalls the remark about the "poverty of values" in *Our God's Brother*.

8. I say: "careful and prayerful reading." No doubt Francis Bacon's ebullient reading was based upon the same text. But Bacon's maxim, "Knowledge is Power," was understood by him—if somewhat ambivalently—to be power exercised within the pattern of the forms of nature, so that in order to overcome nature one needed to follow it. Once the biblical conditions are forgotten, however, Bacon's maxim leads to a ruthless pursuit of indiscriminate power and of absolute control determined by human wish, want, and will. As Gabriel Marcel warned us, absolute power in human hands easily comes to be turned against man himself (see the discussion of the techniques of degradation in *L'homme contre le humain*, translated as *Man against Mass Society* [Chicago: Henry Regnery, 1952]).

9. See the present pope's three encyclicals on this theme: *Laborem Exercens* (On Human Work, 1981), *Sollicitudo Rei Socialis* (On Social Concern, 1987), and *Centesimus Annus* (On the Hundredth Anniversary of *Rerum Novarum*, 1991).

the creation of man (Gen. 2:7–25), John Paul characterizes it as an anthropological account, which gives us what he calls the "subjective definition of man" (*OU* S/19/79, 1; 27). Now, this is perhaps a surprising characterization that has not a little to do with his philosophical background and habitus; for he arrives at the characterization because of the interior quality he finds in the Yahwist account or at least running just under the surface of the account. If the first account had a certain cosmic majesty in its proportions, this older account possesses drama and intimacy. For God is depicted, in anthropomorphic fashion, as walking in the garden of Eden during the cool of the day and asking questions of Adam and Eve as though He did not know the answers. No doubt, this gives to the account its dramatic and intimate flare; but there is more here than what John Paul calls its "primitive mythical character" (*OU* S/19/79, 1; 28). Indeed, John Paul finds the Yahwist text to have even more depth in certain aspects than the more reflective Priestly account. It is interesting that, in maintaining the indissolubility of marriage, Christ refers to the Yahwist text even more emphatically than to the Priestly text, since the Yahwist gives the reason for the indissolubility.[10]

What is more, in an anthropological sense the older account is more complete, since the account details the transition from man's innocence to man's Fall. It is significant, too, that Christ takes his questioners back before the Fall to the innocence of man and affirms the indissolubility of marriage, not only in that state of innocence, but in the present state as well. In this way, Christ bridges the two states. Referring to the Mosaic bill of divorce, Christ says: "It was not so from the beginning" (Matt. 19:8). This proscription of divorce is undoubtedly a hard saying, especially in a society such as ours in which so many families are touched by the pain of divorce in one way or another. We have seen how the dramatist Wojtyła has shown compassion in *The Jeweler's Shop* for couples separated and divorced. But without gainsaying that compassion, John Paul points out that in his reply to the Pharisees, Christ re-

10. See n. 2.

affirms "the principle of the unity and indissolubility of marriage as the very content of the Word of God, expressed in the most ancient revelation" (OU S/5/79, 3; 17). This affirmation regarding marriage is in fact a re-affirmation; it is a reaffirmation of the original intention of the Creator in creating man. It is, then, an affirmation that the original intention still holds and that God's original creative plan gives definition to the very nature of man; it reassures us that our human nature has survived the Fall. To be sure, human nature is wounded terribly by the original sin, but it is not destroyed. The fundamentals, the outlines, the essentials of what it means to be human still remain. That is why the text still has something to tell us today of the origin, nature, and intended destiny of man, and why this most ancient revelation lies at the very root of Christian anthropology, even as the Incarnation of Christ crowns its height.

John Paul calls the Yahwist text "the most ancient description and record of man's self-knowledge, . . . the first testimony of human conscience . . . [which] provides us *in nucleo* with nearly all the elements of the analysis of man, to which modern, and especially contemporary philosophical anthropology is sensitive" (OU S/19/79, 1; 28). This is, indeed, an astounding claim, not least for a text that is thousands of years old and that (along with Genesis 1) carries us back to the very beginning of time. It is an astounding claim, too, for an author who—prior to being elected pope—had concentrated many of his writings precisely on philosophical anthropology in the contemporary manner. It is on this ground, however, that John Paul calls upon us to "try to penetrate towards that 'beginning'" to which Christ called attention by affirming the indissolubility of the married relationship between man and woman (OU S/5/79, 5; 18). Nor is the point of small matter, since that relationship lies in the very womb of the race.

The Yahwist account also takes up not only the making of man ('ādām: man in his original solitude), but it also takes up the making of man ('îš) and woman ('iššâ) in their togetherness. The Priestly account had simply announced: "He created them [i.e., man: 'ādām] male (zākār) and female (něqēbâ)." This fits the cosmological focus on the role of man in the created world: he is to fructify and to subdue the earth. The Yahwist account, on the other hand, being more anthropological in character, makes much of this distinction of gender within the original unity of man (ʾādām).

John Paul insists that it is most important to recognize that the original unity of man is in no way broken up by this distinction into gender. You will recall that God paraded the various kinds of animals before the man (ʾādām) and that the man named them. In so doing, the man identified them and assumed his stewardship over them; that is, he defined his relationship to them. So far, so good. But none of them sufficed to meet either Adam's or God's expectations. ʾādām remained in solitude; but the Yahwist account reads at that point: "It is not good for man to be alone." Something essential is missing; something more is still needed to round out and to complete the origin and nature of man.

Before considering what more is needed, John Paul draws out the deeper meaning of the original solitude of ʾādām, which—John Paul remarks—poses "a fundamental anthropological problem" (OU O/10/79, 3; 45). The original solitude certainly marks man off from the rest of creation: it registers a radical difference between him and other visible creatures, and seals his distinctive nature. For ʾādām alone of all visible creatures has been created in a special way as bearing the image and likeness of God. At this point in his commentary, John Paul remarks that the root of self-knowledge is to be found here in this solitary awareness, which senses both the privilege of the solitude that sets man apart from other creatures, and the incompleteness that attends ʾādām as he faces the rest of the visible creation. John Paul suggests that the double sense of solitude marks man's subjectivity, in contrast to the more objective, cosmic Priestly account in which man is situated at the apex of the visible creation. Indeed, without explicitly elaborating the concept, one might dare to say that in and through this distinctive, original solitude man grasps himself as a person before God. His self-knowledge consists in grasping his reality as a person more than in defining the concept. But it is not too much to say that later thinkers will recognize in this original solitude and in this incipient subjectivity the intimate mark of "incommunicability," which is a distinctive feature of personhood.[11]

And yet the person of 'adām was not fulfilled in this solitude, though it had not yet become that loneliness explored so dramatically in *Radiation of Fatherhood*. The original solitude is not sufficient; man—that is to say, the human being—is not meant to be alone. Still, his very solitude is the seal of God's special relationship; and so it is irrevocable. In resolving this paradox, God breaks open the original solitude, not from without, as the parade of animals had failed to do, but from within humanity itself. May we not say: God breaks into his human creature through that very fissure which Adam so begrudgingly admires in *Radiation of Fatherhood*? Now, even after God's intervention, the original solitude remains as the distinctive mark of the only being whom God has created "for itself," as possessing the inherent dignity of being made in God's own image. But now the solitude is to be fulfilled from within. The solitude that distinguishes man from other creatures remains, but man will receive appropriate filling from within that solitude. And so, God forms another being who possesses that same mark of solitude which bears the image and likeness of God: He fashions Woman.

At this point 'ādām undergoes a double recognition. Upon waking from his induced sleep (for God alone has made the Woman), the man exclaims: "This now at last is bone of my bones and flesh of my flesh!" (Gen. 2:23). Here at last is both helpmate and companion, a being like himself bearing the image and likeness of God. From which the inference is drawn: "Therefore, a man shall leave father and mother, and shall cleave to his wife; and they shall become one flesh [one body]" (Gen 2:24). Even though Scripture is too profound and original to be either a technical or a systematic writing, it is perhaps significant that the Yahwist text at this point

11. Richard of St. Victor in the twelfth century defined person as the "incommunicable existence of a spiritual nature [*spiritualis naturae incommunicabilis existentia*]." (*De Trinitate* 4: 21; Migne, Patrologia Latina, vol. 196, 945.) Cf. St. Thomas Aquinas, *Summa theologiae* I, 29, 3 ad4.

(2:22–24) shifts from the generic term for man (*'ādām*) to the word for man in the masculine sense (*'îš*) and for man in the feminine sense (*'iššâ*).[12]

By any standard, the revelation is momentous, for it discloses that man as male comes to a new self-awareness and self-realization only with the coming into being of man as female. And since the self-awareness and self-realization come about within the distinctive solitude of humanity and with the emergence of another human being within that solitude, the process of self-recognition occurs in the woman as well. A new reciprocity is born within humanity—it is the internal reciprocity of solitudes—and with this inner reciprocity, humanity now acquires its essential completeness. Man and woman are now companionate. She has been formed as helpmate suited to him. This "suitability" rests upon the radical equality of man and woman, which in turn rests upon the fact that each shares in the original and abiding theological relationship: upon having been made in the image of God and according to his likeness. Only on that basis and that equality can *'ādām* cry out: "At last . . . bone of my bones and flesh of my flesh!"[13]

Now, as I have said, John Paul draws our attention to a double recognition, which must yet be explicated. If the first moment of that recognition is the burst of surprise on confronting another human within a shared unity, "bone of my bones, and flesh of my flesh," the second moment consists in the recognition of otherness.

---

12. In English, as in some other languages, the one word "man" does double duty: it serves for the generic and comprehensive sense of man in general (humanity), while it also serves the specific sense in special contexts to denote the masculine or male form of humanity. Latin, on the other hand, for example, has available to it *homo* and *vir*. It should be said, however, that the usage is not systematically observed in the Bible. Still, it is suggestive.

13. And in the New Testament (RSV), St. Paul echoes the old while singing a new song: "Neither Jew nor Greek, neither slave nor free, neither male nor female; for you are all one in Christ Jesus" (Gal. 3:28). None of these distinctions, whether valid or not, override the equal humanity that is defined by the image-relationship to God and by the new freedom in Christ. See John Paul II, *Mulieris Dignitatem: On the Dignity and Vocation of Women*, Vatican translation (Boston: St. Paul Books & Media, n.d.), esp. III, 22ff.

Indeed, the biblical word for "suitable for him" (*neged* from *nā-gad*: to stand in front of, hence to face) suggests another person standing before him, confronting him; hence a "counterpart." For this is not just the recognition of any sort of otherness. The requirement of suitability stipulates a specific kind of counterpart, a specifically correlative counterpart, a counterpart within the same species; and the specification "male and female" makes this clear, hence: a mate.[14] Not until God made man male and female did man in his humanity break out of himself within that same humanity; break out, in and through the knowledge of another being—at once similar to yet different from himself. And with that recognition, the man came to a fuller sense of himself and to a more complete and mutual sense of his humanity (*OU* o/10/79, 5–6; 47–48). Now, precisely the other as female is different from him as male, and, as John Paul emphasizes, that difference includes a visible difference, a difference of body, a difference in the way in which each—the man and the woman—holds their shared humanity.

At a number of points in his catechesis John Paul calls attention to the richness of the biblical texts—and in particular this text from Genesis—for a theology of the body and of human sexuality. It is equally important to notice that here for the first time we have humanity as the original community of persons (*communio personarum*) (*OU* N/14/79, 2; 71). Here then is found the human root of community and sociality. But here too in that same root is found the intimacy and interiority that have been so profoundly reflected upon in the pre-papal writings of Karol Wojtyła.[15] John Paul pauses at this point to stress the matter: "In a relatively few sentences the ancient text portrays man as a person with the subjectivity that characterizes him" (*OU* o/24/79, 1; 50–51). In a

14. The biblical word for "helper" here (*'ēzer*) means to aid, without necessarily implying subjugation. The all too frequent history of domination is part of the pattern of sinfulness.

15. See *Love and Responsibility* and *The Acting Person*, but also numerous articles in Polish, some of which have appeared in English in *Analecta Husserliana* to which I have referred. (See also the bibliography.)

word, the subjectivity of original solitude is complete only as intersubjectivity; and this communion comprises the original unity of man and woman.

The twofold task that is given to the man and the woman—that of parenthood and of stewardship—rests upon the theological relationship: being in the image and likeness of God. First, as to the command to multiply, John Paul remarks that "procreation is rooted in creation" (*OU* N/21/79, 4; 83). Second, both man and woman have been given the task of stewardship on the basis of their image-relation to God and their concomitant mutual self-knowledge; but that task of stewardship supposes the freedom that is part of their likeness to God. And so, along with self-knowledge comes the self-possession, self-determination, and self-governance so emphasized in *The Acting Person* as part of the ontological structure of man. Or, to use the language of metaphysics, human nature is constituted (in part) of intellect and will, of understanding and freedom (*OU* O/24/79, 1; 51). For man's conditional stewardship is to be taken up freely: to subdue the earth, and to till and keep the garden. In Genesis 3, to be sure, we learn how man has mismanaged his freedom. Though, as John Paul points out, not without God offering even then a promise of better days: for God promises that the woman's offspring will in time crush the head of the evil serpent (Gen. 3:15).

John Paul returns more than once to consider the original solitude which, to his mind, holds the riches of the mystery of creation and the relationship with God (*OU* N/21/79, 1; 78–79). Is it too much to see in this original solitude a revelation of that interiority that comes to philosophical expression as reflexive consciousness in *The Acting Person,* and in which is rooted our inner freedom and our capability for transcendence? For is not reflexive consciousness, after all, Wojtyła's philosophical correlate of that original solitude which is the most interior part of human nature? Now, that original solitude is not meant to be solitary. For we have learned from both accounts in Genesis that "the study of the human identity of the one who, at the beginning is 'alone,' must always pass through duality, [into] 'communion'" (*OU* N/21/79, 1;

78). We have already seen, at the close of *The Acting Person,* Karol Wojtyła's reflections on who is my neighbor, in which we are called upon to recognize our opportunity for solidarity with others. But the beginnings of that solidarity must pass through the duality of gender by passing through the intersubjectivity of masculine and feminine: "male and female He made them." For these are, John Paul continues,

two "incarnations" of the same metaphysical solitude, before God and the world—two ways, as it were, of "being a body," and at the same time [of being] a man, [two ways] which complete each other—two complementary dimensions, as it were, of self-consciousness and self-determination, and, at the same time, two complementary ways of being conscious of the meaning of the body.

It should be noticed that this meaning is embedded in the utterly concrete forms of "he" or "she."

Now, these elements of human experience are present in everyday experience as the original constituents of human subjectivity. The Bible, however, draws our attention to what modern scholars of religion have called the "numinous," that is, to "the extraordinary side of what is ordinary" (*OU* D/12/79, 1; 85–86). The numinous is associated with the divine, and the Yahwist now mentions an emotion all too familiar to the human. Or rather, the Yahwist first mentions its absence in the state of paradisal innocence. For "the man and woman were both naked, and were not ashamed" (Gen. 2:25). The original nakedness brought with it no shame, though we may be sure that a purer form of numinous awe was present.

At this point, John Paul observes that it is not possible for historical man—that is, for us who experience both fallenness and the promise of redemption—to experience directly that first innocence (*OU* D/112/79, 4; 88). Still, we ought not to leave this impossibility entirely untouched, for the biblical text tells us something of ourselves and our present state that is continuous with the former state of innocence.[16] As we pass from innocence to the

16. This is the point of beginning with Christ's affirmation of what holds "from the beginning" (see n. 2).

Fall we enter the sphere of shame. After having committed the sin, the man and the woman try to hide their nakedness, for they were ashamed: "I was afraid, because I was naked, and I hid myself" (Gen. 3:10). The covert action filled with shame stands in marked contrast to the preceding innocent nakedness and its lack of shame. John Paul identifies the original nakedness of our first parents, nakedness without shame, with the original innocence of the original solitude. The shame of nakedness, on the other hand, marks a limit situation. The experience of shame is a boundary experience; by that very fact, it can throw a dark light upon this side of our human condition, but, with the help of this most ancient revelation, the experience of shame can also adumbrate that original condition (OU D/12/79, 4; 89). While John Paul recognizes that we cannot in our present situation undergo the actual experience of innocence, yet he probes that condition by means of a revelation-assisted reconstruction of it.[17]

The terminology of "limit situation" and "boundary experience" discloses John Paul's philosophical background. In the philosophical movement with which he is in some sense allied—that is, modern phenomenology—a boundary experience does not actually carry us over to direct contact with what lies on the other side of that from which we have come, but it does indirectly point to it and bring us closer to it. Thus, we have direct experience of shame, but not of innocence. And yet, the experience of shame is somehow connected with innocence. For there would be no shame without the memory of (lost) innocence. This connectedness undoubtedly accounts for the tension and confusion that are the hallmarks of shame. To be sure, we directly experience the one but not the other; but a boundary is not simply a wall. The experience adumbrates that other side, shadows it forth, after the manner of one of those devices that permit us to look indirectly upon a bright eclipse without enabling us to look directly at it. Through the ex-

17. Cf. *Love and Responsibility*, trans. from the 2d and 3d Polish editions (New York: Farrar, Straus, Giroux, 1981), pp. 174–93, which takes up the "metaphysics of shame," the "law of the absorption of shame by love," and the "problem of shamelessness" [see Grondelski, item 84].

perience of shame, which we can share with our first parents, we can be carried back—not *to* or even *into* that sphere of innocence, but carried, if I may so put it—back *at* the beginning, back to the threshold of something that is not directly accessible to us. John Paul further suggests that with the help of the biblical text, and from the border-experience of shame, we can reconstruct something of the original human state, something that tells us about ourselves, our nature, and our intended destiny. Thus, for example, we can draw from the text (Gen. 3 and following) the knowledge that shame registers a loss of an original fullness, and particularly as it affects the body (*OU* D/19/79, 2; 94).

To recapitulate: These opening chapters of Genesis articulate a number of themes precious to our own understanding of humanity and to the proper use of our freedom. First, they reveal the theological character of man, his imaging of God. Then, they disclose the original solitude which sets man apart from other creatures by virtue of his special relationship to God. After that they reveal the fashioning and discovery of a suitable companion, so that man does not remain alone; moreover, they disclose a companion with a difference. With the distinction of gender or sexuality, there emerges a fresh and developing fullness of mutual self-knowledge, self-determination, and self-realization. And finally, there is told the sad story of the misuse of our freedom and the transition from innocence to guilt, from an original nakedness without shame—openness to God—to the subsequent fear and covertness experienced as shame.

Shame is not only a confusion, however, but also a division, for it possesses a dynamic by which man and woman are driven apart. They are thrown back upon themselves, so that their original solitude becomes a derivative loneliness, derivative from that fateful choice. It is an empty loneliness, the loneliness of dispossession and self-alienation experienced by Anna in *The Jeweler's Shop*; it is the stubborn loneliness preferred by Adam in *Radiation of Fatherhood*. At the same time, however, man and woman are still drawn together toward that original unity in various, if often distorted, ways. And so, the original unity is never wholly lost, but neither is it ever wholly recovered in the present state (*OU* D/19/ 79, 1; 92–93). The original solitude remains, but it has been tainted by alienation, refracted by isolation from the other, and made painful by residual loneliness.

Having broken with the original openness to God, it is not accidental that the first experience of shame is an interior tremor. It is a tremor that exposes itself in the very act of attempting to hide. Original sin, then, brings about the first transparent cover-up. The cover-up is experienced as shame because it is known or suspected by all parties to be transparent. It is the primordial dissemblance that in its futility manifests itself.

To this most ancient of the revelations given to us—the revelation of our original innocence, our fall and shame, and the promise of our redemption—a Christian anthropology must return. In meditating upon this revelation we place ourselves at the very source and beginning of our humanity, the primordial *communio personarum*; for what is revealed to us here once was so. And the revelation therefore remains our surest access to what God originally intended for us. We need then to continue to contemplate the mystery held within that revelation, even as we meditate upon the brilliant mystery of Christ, Who redeemed the original promise in an unprecedented and wholly gratuitous way. For in his incarnation, suffering, and resurrection, He continues to shed his light upon the human nature that He shares with us.

∽

Of course, to present John Paul II's Christology in any adequate way lies beyond the scope of the present undertaking and might in any case better left to a properly theological exposition.[18] Nevertheless, we might with benefit join his papal *Discorsi* on the origins of man with earlier aspects of his pastoral mission. For it is a mission already begun by the young Father Wojtyła and raised to diocesan scope when he became bishop and then archbishop of Cracow. It assumed a wider sphere as he became council father

18. A thorough consideration of John Paul's theological anthropology would entail an exposition of the later *Christological Catecheses*, given during the years 1987–88 and appearing in the English edition of *Osservatore Romano*.

and cardinal and reached its apex in the office of supreme pastor. That mission is grounded in an ecclesiology that, along with his anthropology, is rooted in Christ. Ever since the Second Vatican Council he has sought to follow its spirit and direction, especially as outlined in the two major documents of that council: The Dogmatic Constitution on the Church (*Lumen gentium*) and the Pastoral Constitution on the Church in the Modern World (*Gaudium et spes*).[19]

Indeed, the outlines of his ecclesiology are already discernible in the contributions he made during the Second Vatican Council as a member of the Polish delegation. Some brief attention to his interventions will highlight his sense of mission.[20] What is most telling from a philosophical perspective is his repeated insistence that all aspects of life are related to and grounded in the truth, and specifically in the truth embodied in, revealed by, and flowing from Christ. Because of the comprehensive and ultimate character of that truth, he will find it entirely appropriate in his papal mission to insist that all people, and not only believers, are to be addressed by the Church. Indeed, we find this emphasis upon the universal significance of the Christian message, upon its inherent catholicity, already present in an intervention he made during the

19. The Latin documents are available in *I Documenti del Concilio Vaticano II*, Edizione Paoline. English translations are to be found in *Vatican Council II: The Conciliar and Post-Conciliar Documents*, ed. Austin Flannery, O.P. (Collegeville, Minn.: Liturgical Press, 1975); also in *Documents of Vatican II*, ed. W. M. Abbott and J. Gallagher (New York: Association Press, 1966), as well as in individual editions. See Karol Wojtyła, *Sources of Renewal. The Implementation of the Second Vatican Council* (Polish ed., 1972; English [from the rev. Italian ed. 1979] (London: Collins [Fount], 1980). Upon his installation as Metropolitan Archbishop of Cracow, he declared his intention to implement the teachings of the council: "Things eternal, things of God, are very simple and very profound. We don't have to create new programmes; we have to find new ways, new energies and a new enthusiasm for sharing in the eternal plan of God and of Christ, and of fulfilling it in the context of our times. The council has set things in motion, but for many of us its decrees are as yet merely written documents. I want to awaken the archdiocese of Cracow to the true meaning of the council, so that we may bring its teaching into our lives" (quoted by Mary Craig in *Man from a Far Country* [London: Hodder and Stoughton, 1979], p. 106). [A glance at the Grondelski bibliography shows more than a dozen items directly engaging the thought and spirit of Vatican II.]

20. For a listing of some of his interventions during the council, see Grondelski, Part III.

Second Vatican Council.[21] Before the council had begun, in response to the commission preparing for the council, he had recommended that the provisional document should put more emphasis upon what reconciles men to the Church rather than what separates them from it.[22]

And what is this truth that is received, nourished, and proclaimed by the Church? It is nothing other than the Mystical Body of Christ present in the world. In a critique of the provisional schema *De Ecclesia,* he wrote that the Mystical Body of Christ should not be put forward merely as one of several images of the Church. The Mystical Body of Christ is more than an image: it is the defining aspect of the Church under its Christological aspect.[23] The Church, then, ought to be presented as the mystery that it is, the mystery revealed by the trinitarian God.[24] In keeping with the mystery of the Church and its pastoral mission, the sacramental efficacy of its liturgy needs to be emphasized.[25] But also in keeping

---

21. For his interventions in the council, see *Acta Synodalis Sacrosancti Concilii Oecumenici Vaticani Secundi,* Periodo III, pars 2; Periodo IV, pars 2 (Typis Polyglottis Vaticanum 1972); hereafter *AS.* During the council and in the context of a discussion on ecumenism and religious liberty, Wojtyła speaks of the "full and solid truth about man" provided by the light of faith, which is awaited by both believers and non-believers: "Hanc veritatem exspectant tam credentes quam etiam non credentes" (*AS* III-2, 5, 532).—I am indebted to Fr. Stephen Digiovanni for drawing my attention to Wojtyła's several contributions to the conciliar deliberations. Cf. John Paul II, *The Whole Truth About Man* (To University Faculties and Students), ed. James Schall, S.J. (Boston: St. Paul Editions, 1981).

22. See *Acta et Documenta Concilio Oecumenico Vaticano II Apparando,* Series I (Antepraeparatoria), Vol. II, Part 2 (Typis Polyglottis Vaticanum, 1960); hereafter *AD.* For this and other recommendations, see Wojtyła's ample response (Dec. 30, 1959, in *AD* II-2, 32, 741–48), and in particular, concerning those separated from the Church by reason of heresy or schism (see 743): "minorem accentum praebendo his omnibus, quae separant, quaerendo autem omnia quae conciliant."

23. See *AS* II-3, 103, 857: "plus est quam imago—est enim determinatio ipsius naturae Ecclesiae sub aspectu christologico et simul sub aspectu mysteriorum Incarnationis et Redemptionis."

24. Indeed, in discussing revelation he puts the issue strongly. The origin (*origo*) of revelation is to be found "not in Tradition or Scripture but solely in God speaking." And if we do call Scripture and Tradition "sources" (*fontes*), the word *fons* is said improperly and secondarily of them, and is to be said of them only according to the analogy of attribution and in respect to the primary analogate, God (*AS* I-3, 15, 294). In discussing the preparatory schema *De Ecclesia,* he finds too little stress upon the mystery of salvation (*AS* I-4, 82, 598).

25. *AS* I-2, 13, 314–15.

with the mystery of its origins, the document on the Church (the provisional schema *de Ecclesia*) needs to show the intimate connection of the Blessed Virgin Mary with the Church; it needs to show her as composite with the Church, not juxtaposed to it.[26]

Wojtyła further urged that the same document should give clearer expression to the communal nature of the Church. And so, the document should first present the Church as the people of God, and only then should the hierarchy of states of life within the Church be presented, and presented as ordered to the common good of the whole people. In this way the whole Church—the college of bishops united with the supreme pastor, the clergy, laity, and religious—can be seen as a dynamic reality ordered toward its own finality: the call to holiness.[27] For the work of the Church is one: to proclaim Christ.

In a joint appeal to Pope Paul VI, signed with other council fathers, Wojtyła expressed his general satisfaction with what was then known as Schema XIII: The Church in the Modern World (*Gaudium et spes*).[28] He went even further in his own name, saying

26. *AS* III-2, 51, 178–79: "Cum tamen caput illud [i.e., on the Blessed Virgin] est ultimum in schemate [*De Ecclesia*], doctrina in ipso contenta magis videtur iuxta-posita quam composita doctrinae totius schematis, magis apparet ut aliquod corollarium quam ut pars."—And again, on behalf of the Polish bishops, *AS* II-3, 103, 856–57: "tunc [i.e., if the tractate on the Virgin is tacked on to the end of the document] doctrina in eo [i.e., in the present form of the schema] contenta videretur esse aliquid supplementarium, et forsitan artificialiter adnexum doctrinae illius schematis. . . ." Instead, the true and intimate connexion (*intima connexio*) of Mary with the Church should be made more evident): "Talis connexio Matris Christi cum Ecclesia sub aspectu maternitatis postulat alium pro hac doctrina locum in schemate, non ultimum." Nor does this preclude other aspects of Mariology (*AS* II-3, 103, 857).—On Mary as *mediatrix*, see *AS* I-4, 82, 598–99.

27. On the *populus Dei*, and the hierarchical structure as instrumentum bonum commune totius populi Dei, and for the divisione communitatis ecclesiasticae per status, i.e. per clericos, laicos et religiosos, see *AS* II-3, 5, 154–55. And he remarks (*AS* II-4, 128, 340) that the provisional schema De Ecclesia treats of the efficient, formal, and material causes of the Church, but says nothing or little about its finality, which is *vocatio ad sanctitatem*.—On collegiality, see *AS* III-1, 33, 613–17. On the growth of an active laity, he remarks on the need among the clergy for a recognition of the contemporary shift in social relations from the older patriarchal relationships to more democratic ones, and yet the need to maintain that sense of paternity or fatherhood that is essential to the care of souls (*AD* II-2, 32, 743). On the apostolate of the laity, see *AS* III-4, 5, 69–70; *AS* III-4, 12, 788–89.—On the religious life, see *AD* II-2, 32, 747.

28. *AS* III-5, 48, 508–9: "il se présente à nous comme un heureux complé-

that the absence of such a document would be a great loss to both the Church and the world.[29] He remarked upon the complexity of the world which the Church must address, *haec pluralitas 'mundorum' in unico mundo,* finding in the original schema an insufficient recognition of this complexity. But more important still, he urged that the Church take up the problems of the world not only as teaching with authority but also with a readiness to inquire with the world into the difficult problems of contemporary human life. In that way the schema would not turn out to be a soliloquy.[30] What is needed, he told the council fathers, is dialogue with the world.[31]

The call to dialogue arises out of Wojtyła's understanding of man as a person called to truth by the person of Christ. In his response to the preparatory commission of the council, Wojtyła underlined the importance of Christian personalism. He urged that it be clearly distinguished from other personalisms and from other anthropologies, such as atheistic materialism and secular humanism.[32] Warning against religious individualism, in an inter-

---

ment du schéma 'de Ecclesia.' . . . [Then, in arguing for more time in arriving at the final version of the proposed Schema XIII on the Church in the Modern World, the several fathers call the proposed schema] un schéma aussi nouveau et aussi difficile."

29. *AS* III-5, 12, 298: After expressing the agreement of the Polish bishops with the general principles of the schema, he continues: "Liceat mihi dicere, quod absentia talis schematis magno esset detrimento tam Ecclesiae quam mundi."

30. *Ibid.,* 299–300: "non tantum modo auctoritativo, sed etiam simul cum ipso inquirere veram et aequam solutionem difficilium problematum vitae humanae. . . . Caveamus autem, ne schema nostrum soliloquium fiat!" And he adds that Schema XIII "is not only for the world outside the Church, but also for the Church in the world—or rather in the different 'worlds' to which we have alluded."

31. Specifically, he finds the chapter on marriage and the family in the provisional schema inadequate, not in its doctrine but in the way in which it approaches the actual contemporary condition of married life: Non agitur de corpore doctrinae, sed de modo loquendi. The approach should be dialogical: *sub aspectu pastorali.* (*AS* IV-3, 67, 242). His interventions during the council were followed by his establishing a Family Institute in the Archdiocese of Cracow. In 1981 as pope he issued the apostolic exhortation *Familiaris Consortio: The Role of the Christian Family in the Modern World* (Boston: St. Paul Editions). [For his writings on marriage and the family, see Grondelski, part II, section D.]

32. He remarks that the growth of various materialisms (as well as of individualism) needs to be confronted by Christian personalism, which understands man as a free moral agent: "The human person as a supposit acting freely and with

vention concerning the schema *De Ecclesia*, Wojtyła remarked that the human person constitutes the cell (*cellulam*) of the Church which, as the Mystical Body of Christ, is a true society.[33] In being called to participate in that holiness which is the Holy Trinity, the Church itself is called to holiness in the persons of its members (*sanctitas Ecclesiae in personis humanis*).[34] This emphasis upon the person extends even to the way in which we use language concerning essential human values.[35] The emphasis upon the person opened up for Wojtyła a personalist approach to natural law, which enabled him to break through the modern dichotomy between what is natural and what is human and to enhance the personal character of traditional natural law.[36] In the conciliar debates concerning religious liberty, Wojtyła gave expression to his understanding of the relation between freedom, truth, and the human person.[37] In the ecumenical context, he stressed the link between liberty and truth, since all Christians are to seek the truth that liberates believers from schism and for union. In the words of Christ, the truth will set you free (John 8:32), and without *that*

---

conscience includes in his acts a moral dimension" (*AD* II-2, 32, 741–42).—For his intervention concerning the problem of atheism (touching as well on ethical relativism and utilitarianism) and the state of the question, see *AS* IV-2, 14, 661–63.

33. *AS* I-4, 82, 598.

34. *AS* II-4, 128, 340–41 (with citations from St. Thomas on the notion of sanctity).

35. Wojtyła warns against a merely "instrumental" use of language neglectful of a true hierarchy of values, and he advocates a consciously personalist mode of communication in keeping with the principle of Christian personalism (*AS* I-3, 43, 609).

36. See, for example, numerous essays in *Von der Königswürde des Menschen*, ed. J. Stroynowski (Stuttgart-Degerloch: Seewald, 1980), esp. "Die anthropologische Vision der Enzyklika *Humanae Vitae*," pp. 177–202, and "Die menschliche Person und das Naturrecht," pp. 59–64. See also "Die ethische Fibel" in *Erziehung zur Liebe* (Seewald, 1980), esp. "Das Gesetz der Natur," pp. 93–98; also in the same collection, "Gedanken über die Ehe," pp. 43–61, which takes up the topics "the foundations of personalism," "the culture of the person," and "the economy and personalism."

37. His insistence upon the objective nature of truth (as well as its subjective aspect) (see *AS* III-3, 51, 766 and elsewhere) is in complete harmony with his recommendation concerning the formation of the clergy: that they be given not only a moral formation but a properly intellectual one as well: *non tantum formatio moralis sed etiam intellectualis* (*AD* I-2, 32, 745).

truth there is no Christian liberty: *Non datur libertas sine veritate.*
That is why something more positive than tolerance is needed in
relations between separated Christians; what is needed is charity.
For tolerance leaves us with no more than the present status quo,
whereas Christians need to advance together toward nothing less
than the truth that frees believers from division.[38]

In considering the civil, juridical, or political sense of religious
liberty, Wojtyła asked that the ethical sense of liberty be clearly
distinguished from the civil sense. The latter rests upon the former,[39] and the ethical sense contains within it a responsibility toward the truth.[40] For the moment of liberty resides in the choice,
not just of any good but of the true good; and the perfection of
the human person is to be found in that truth.[41] He acknowledged
that, in the matter of civil liberty, it is in the interest of religious
believers to urge mutual tolerance as a fundamental social right
(*jus*). But he went on to say that not even civil liberty is founded
on the principle of tolerance alone, for it is more deeply grounded
in the natural right of everyone to (be free to come to) know the
truth.[42] In affirming the right of religious liberty, the Church ought
not to speak only of civil tolerance; it ought rather to put forward
its own full sense of the liberty communicated to it by Christ, and
to put it forward as a revealed doctrine that is consonant with
sound human reason even as it transcends that reason.[43] For the
right to religious liberty is drawn from the dignity of the human
person in conformity with truth and justice.[44] Bearing in mind, no

38. *AS* III-2, 5, 531. In distinguishing liberty from tolerance, he remarks that
the principle of an invincibly erroneous conscience is only the religious formulation
of the principle of tolerance (*AS* III-2, 22, 838), and as such it is partial and negative
(*AS* III-3, 51, 766). On the more positive "making truth in charity," see *AS* III-3,
51, 766–68.
39. *AS* III-3, 51, 766; also *AS* III-2, 5, 530f.; and *AS* III-2, 22, 838.
40. *AS* IV-2, 1, 11–13: *Non tantum dicere "in hac re* (i.e., in the matter of
religious liberty) *liber sum," sed etiam "responsabilis sum."*
41. *AS* III-3, 766.
42. *AS* III-3, 51, 766. Cf. *AS* III-2, 22, 838–39; *AS* III-2, 5, 531–32.
43. *AS* IV-2, 112, 293. Touching the question of Christian philosophy, it is
interesting to notice that Wojtyła here urges that the rational concept of religious
liberty be presented as contained within the revealed doctrine, since the council is
to teach divine, and not only human, truth.
44. *AS* IV-2, 112, 293. As the title of the second chapter of the document on

doubt, the harassment of the Church under the then-Communist regimes, as well as other hostile regimes, Wojtyła insisted upon the transcendent character of the religious search for truth. It is a search that seeks nothing less than the relation of the person to God, a relation in which no secular power is entitled to intervene.[45] Nevertheless, the Church ought to approach the secular powers in a spirit of dialogue and with mutual respect, even while it addresses the whole of mankind.

∽

If we turn again to his papal writings, talks and travels, we see that he has taken his own advice seriously. In his mission as pope he has continued to address all mankind and to call all Christians to witness. Indeed, the role of witness is intrinsic to the faith of Christians, for whom there can be no substitute for the personal and collective truth about man revealed by the unique and universal person of Christ. In keeping with Wojtyła's earlier conciliar call to dialogue, John Paul underlines the conditions of witness and mission. They are the conditions of dialogue: openness to others, respect for sincere opinions, and the intention to propose Christ rather than to impose oneself on others[46] (*RMi* 1; 7–8; I, 4; 12; IV, 39; 60).

Thus, in the discussion of concrete social and economic problems, he insists that "the Church has no models to present"[47] (*CA*

---

religious liberty Wojtyła suggested: "The Doctrine of Religious Liberty Grounded (*fundata*) in the Dignity of the Human Person" (*AS* IV-2, 1, 11).—The final text of the *Declaration* reads: "It is in accordance with their dignity that all men, because they are persons, that is, beings endowed with reason and free will and therefore bearing personal responsibility, are both impelled by their nature and bound by a moral obligation to seek the truth, especially religious truth" (*Dignitatis Humanae*, chap. I, no. 2; *Vatican Council II*, ed. Austin Flannery, O.P., p. 801).

45. *AS* III-2, 5, 532.

46. *Redemptoris Missio*, Introduction, sections 1–2, pp. 7–8; hereafter cited in the body of the text as *RMi* with part, then section, and after the semicolon the page from *The Mission of Christ the Redeemer*, Vatican translation (Sherbrooke, Quebec: Editions Paulines, 1991). The English translation of many of John Paul II's papal statements are available in inexpensive editions by the Daughters of St. Paul. I will use a similar code for other papal documents.

47. *Centesimus Annus: The Social Teaching of the Church*, Vatican translation (Sherbrooke, Quebec: Editions Paulines, 1991); hereafter *CA* in the body of the text.

IV, 43; 77ff.); but it does offer to all men a hymn to the new life brought by Christ (*RMi* I, 7; 16; also I, 9; 19). And in presenting Christ it is empowered to draw from Him, and from that human nature with which God created man, principles for the discernment of values and disvalues in the concrete order, principles that include those of traditional natural law. And so, while Christology stands at the head and heart of John Paul's theological anthropology, the philosophical aspect continues to play an indispensable role within his full anthropology.

In their ultimate sense, John Paul II's philosophical ideas function within an essentially theological context, itself centered upon Christ in the Trinity. The most accessible source for that broader and deeper context is provided by his encyclical letters. He has issued eight in all, of which three are given to social topics: The first, issued in 1981, as *Laborem Exercens/On Human Work,* was inspired no doubt by his experience as a worker and by his continuing interest in work as a primary feature of human existence.[48] His second letter on social themes (1987) was more wide-ranging, as its title indicates: *Sollicitudo Rei Socialis/On Social Concern.*[49] The third, issued in 1991, was called for by the centenary commemoration of the great social encyclical of Leo XIII, *Rerum Novarum*; it bears the title: *Centesimus Annus/The Social Teaching of the Church.*[50]

The deeper and broader context is provided, however, by his encyclicals on the central dogmas of the Christian faith. I do not mean thereby, of course, to deny that the social encyclicals also teach, but they teach within the context of the great doctrines of the Christian religion. These doctrinal encyclicals march grandly along the line of fundamental teachings. The first, issued in 1979, centers upon Christ, and is entitled *Redemptor Hominis/The Re-*

48. Vatican Polyglot translation (Boston: St. Paul Editions, n.d.); hereafter cited in the body of the text as *LE.*—It commemorated the ninetieth anniversary of Pope Leo XIII's *Rerum Novarum.*

49. Vatican translation (Boston: St. Paul Books & Media, n.d.); hereafter referred to in the body of the text as *SRS.* It commemorated the twentieth anniversary of Pope Paul VI's *Populorum Progressio.*

50. See n. 47.

deemer of Man.[51] It was followed in 1980 by *Dives in Misericor-dia/On the Mercy of God,* which unfolded a pristine vision of the mystery of the Father's love.[52] In 1986, completing the consideration of the Trinity, came the encyclical on the Holy Spirit, stressing as it did the intimate co-operation of the Spirit with the Word: *Dominum et Vivificantem/On the Holy Spirit in the Life of the Church and the World.*[53] These three great encyclicals were followed in 1987 by an encyclical letter on Mary, *Redemptoris Mater/ Mother of the Redeemer,*[54] attesting to her prominence in the faith of John Paul, the Polish nation, and the universal Church. And in 1990 came an encyclical letter on the missionary mandate given to the Church by Christ: *Redemptoris Missio/The Mission of Christ the Redeemer.*[55]

In his encyclical letters, John Paul II is conscious of following and developing the spirit of the Second Vatican Council, in which, as we have seen, he was an active participant. While he draws upon a range of conciliar documents, and more widely upon Scripture, patristics, theology and the writings of his predecessors in the Holy See, John Paul gives special attention to the constitution *Gaudium et Spes/The Church in the Modern World,* and especially to the famous section 22.[56] He takes as the center of his teaching the conciliar theme that "Christ the New Adam . . . reveals man to himself." This, he tells us, is the keystone of an "authentic humanism" (*RH* II, 9; 19), whose aim is to effect a "mature humanity in each of us" (*RH* IV, 21; 54). The mention of "maturity" takes the word out of the very mouth of the Enlightenment, which means something quite different by it. Through His Incarnation, Christ has entered into history: "God entered the history of humanity and, as a man, became an actor in that history, one of the

51. Vatican Polyglot translation (Boston: St. Paul Editions, n.d.); hereafter *RH*.
52. Vatican Polyglot translation (Boston: St. Paul Editions, n.d.); hereafter *DM*.
53. Vatican translation (Boston: St. Paul Books & Media, n.d.); hereafter *DV*.
54. Vatican translation (Boston: Daughters of St. Paul, n.d.); hereafter *RMa*.
55. See n. 46.
56. "On Christ the New Man," *Gaudium et Spes,* pt. I, chap. 1, sec. 22 (*AAS* 58 [1966], p. 1042; *I Documenti,* pp. 375–78; Abbot, *Vatican II,* 922–24). It forms the very center of his Christian anthropology.

thousands of millions of human beings but at the same time Unique! Through the Incarnation God gave human life the dimension that He intended man to have from his first beginning" (*RH* I, 1; 6). In somewhat startling language, John Paul tells us that Christ thereby accepted "His particular right of citizenship" (*RH* II, 10; 19). It is not surprising that a definite ecclesiology follows from this central doctrine, expressed in the conciliar formula: Man is "the primary and fundamental way for the Church" (*RH* III, 14; 26–27).

In *Dives in Misericordia,* following the teaching of section 22 of *Gaudium et Spes*—that Christ fully reveals man to himself—John Paul draws further upon that teaching: Christ alone fully reveals man to himself, "in the very revelation of the mystery of the Father and His love" (*DM* I, 1; 7–8). The more the Church centers its concern upon man, the more its anthropocentric emphasis upon the confirmation and actualization of man must not be separated from its theocentric source. There can be no true humanism that is not theocentric (*DM* I, 1; 8).

Now, such a teaching is not surprising, especially from the pen of a pope. But *Dives in Misericordia* takes us into deeper waters, in which we reach quite remarkable insights into the depths of God's merciful love. In words reminiscent of *Our God's Brother, The Jeweler's Shop,* and *Radiation of Fatherhood,* the most pronounced theme is that of the unifying and elevating power of merciful love: for mercy brings about the cohesion of intimacy, justice, human dignity, and the creative power of love; it accomplishes this cohesion in and through the actual revelation of the Father's mercy. In *The Acting Person,* Karol Wojtyła described the high point of consciousness to be the task of integration and transcendence. And in *Dives in Misericordia* (*DM* VII, 14; 42), John Paul tells us that love is "a unifying and also an elevating power," precisely the features attendant upon reflexive consciousness, features derived undoubtedly from this very love which is experienced in the form of divine mercy. For in the reign of sin, the Father, who is the inexhaustible power of forgiving love, "*cannot reveal Himself otherwise* than as mercy" (*DM* VII, 13; 40–41). Indeed, we are told that mercy "is, as it were, love's second name" (*DM* V, 7; 26). Its second name: for in the end time, the time of eschatological fulness, "mercy will be revealed as love," but in this time, "love must be revealed above all as mercy and must be actualized as mercy." Now, this intimate relation of love and mercy is also a call to action. In the words of James's epistle (1: 22): "Be doers of the word, and not hearers only."

We have already heard the call to action in the works of Karol Wojtyła: it is the call to full and proper human action, to deliberate acts of the will, grounded in the convertibility of being, truth and the good, and open both to the grace of God and to responsible human creativity. Action, above all, brings to fruition what it means to be human; for it is in acting that we consummate our being. Now, the reality and value of such active witness is not to be grasped narrowly. Consummate action may take form as the quiet acts of prayer, meditation and contemplation open to all conscious beings, and which are of the highest importance and value, attaching us to our transcendent source, and by means of its inner bonds attaching us also to our fellow creatures.

What is more, properly human action in its true nature is action-in-response; it is action founded upon listening to a prior initiative, an initiative registered by our conscience (in the form both of natural law and of revelation). It is also action in response to what one's family and one's culture is saying, to what one's neighbor needs and offers, and in the first place to what God has revealed about the distinctive character and destiny of the race. Action, then, is appropriate response to what has been received.[57] Now, such responsive and responsible action is seldom easy, and

57. If I am not mistaken, the category of receptivity (not understood as passivity, but in the Marcellian sense of that which transcends both ordinary activity and ordinary passivity, as a host "receives" his guest), while it is clearly present and understood to be present in Karol Wojtyła's thought, nevertheless has not received the same diligent analysis from him that the category of action has. The relative emphasis may be accounted for by Wojtyła's concern to retrieve the aspect of action from Scheler's too passive notion of experience. Nevertheless, his continued insistence upon the agent's response to the normative power of the true good and to the truthfulness of conscience obviously places the moral agent in the disposition of receptivity and highlights its supreme importance, to say nothing of the reception of grace from God's mercy.

it often breaks forth into the human arena only after a conscious struggle. That struggle is, above all, not with others, but with one-self and with that fallen human nature that has been embodied as Adam in the dramas.

The emphasis upon action raises the question of the relative value of pure theoretical knowledge as distinguished from practical knowledge. The question asks about genuine theoretical knowledge and not that excessive intellectualism decried in the dramas as "intelligence without love." Is it too much to say that genuine theoretical knowledge also adumbrates—even though it does not recapture—our original innocence? Yet it does seem clear that for Karol Wojtyła/John Paul II, purely theoretical knowledge needs to be completed in some way and at some time by some kind of action: by prayer which maintains a conversation with God, by celebration which increases joy in glory, by teaching which deepens the understanding of truth, by artistic creation which certifies freedom, by productivity which enhances life, or by service which whispers the primacy of love. Such is the substance and the life to which Christ calls each acting person.

CHAPTER V

Taking the Measure
of the Philosophical Project
Modernity Meets Tradition

In conclusion, it remains to draw out some of the essential philosophical elements of the anthropology of Karol Wojtyła/John Paul II for further reflection and evaluation, and to trace their continuing presence in the papal writings. Wojtyła's philosophical project bears within it an affinity with the Second Vatical Council, even though the lines of his own thought were already drawn before the council was even so much as a gleam in the eye of Pope John XXIII. And this affinity is there. It is sometimes said that Karol Wojtyła is a man made by the council. I take this to mean that he came to the notice of the larger world through his activity during the council and that he developed and enriched an approach already underway. For, if he was made by the council, he was also a man ready for the council. Certainly, the direction of his own thought had already been shaped in the years preceding the council. It is not inaccurate to sum up the intention of the council in two words: *aggiornamento* and *ressourcement,* for the council sought to update the Church in continuity with its long tradition. And Wojtyła's philosophical work is very much in this same spirit: to bring new philosophical methods to the service of a fresh understanding of the human person, and in particular, to bring a new light to the traditional understanding of the foundations of ethical action in the concrete moral agent.

In summing up the philosophical character of the enterprise and reflecting upon its viability, it will help to borrow a technique from *The Acting Person,* and to bracket the philosophical aspect; by placing that aspect before the brackets, Karol Wojtyła's philosophy may throw its own light upon the rich complex of John Paul's theological ideas within the brackets (see chap. II, above). It is characteristic of his thought, both as philosopher and as pontiff, to meet the challenge of the modern world directly and confidently. He is not afraid to admit change, even as he takes its measure.

Thus, in his first encyclical, *Redemptor Hominis,* in paying tribute to his recent predecessors and to the Second Vatican Council, John Paul observes that "this [recent] inheritance has struck deep roots in the awareness of the Church *in an utterly new way, quite unknown* previously" (*RH* I, 3; 7; italics added). Many factors, under the guidance of the Holy Spirit, have contributed to this new understanding. Speaking as a philosopher, Karol Wojtyła had already noticed one factor that continues to play a role in present-day consciousness. In an essay which he announced as a concluding supplement to *The Acting Person,*[1] Wojtyła remarked upon the *shift of consciousness* that has occurred during modern times. In *Redemptor Hominis* (*RH* III, 15; 28ff.), John Paul addresses the topic "What modern man is afraid of." And there he calls upon the Church neither wholly to endorse nor wholly to condemn modernity. What Christians must do is to search the ambiguity of the concrete conditions of modern life, and especially in its putative progressive technology, in order to sift out what is for man's genuine good and what is not.

He is not reluctant to appropriate much of the vocabulary and many of the concepts of modernity and to modify them to his purpose. We might take, as an example, his use of the concept and language of rights (*jus*). There can be no doubt of the checkered origin of its modern sense, nurtured by the blood of the first of the modern total revolutions, the French Revolution. Nor can there be any doubt either about its frequent abuse in the service of an individualism that is at best indifferent and at worst hostile to the deepest hopes for man that are nourished by the Church. Nevertheless, the concept has its value.[2] With that in mind, John Paul

1. "The Person: Subject and Community," *Review of Metaphysics* 33, no. 2 (Dec. 1979): 273–308.
2. The Latin term *jus,* used by John Paul as well as by his predecessors, pre-

has used the term in ways that, while they maintain the papal teaching, nevertheless differ from recent papal usage and emphasis. Moreover, the difference is not only in the manner of speaking;[3] the usage also adds a new appreciation for the personal and subjective depth of human reality.

It is not surprising, perhaps, that the terminology has disconcerted some Catholics; and no doubt an indiscriminate and imprecise, unreflective and uncritical use might well contribute to undermining Catholic doctrine by inserting an excessive and irresponsible individualism into its teaching about the constitution of the human person. John Paul's remedy, however, is not simply to avoid the term. On the contrary, in *Laborem Exercens,* he endorses the right to private property, traditionally defended by the social teaching of the church, and he associates that right with the traditional concern for the common good (*LE* III, 14; 34–35).[4] But he speaks there, too, of the rights of the worker as part of the wider range of rights pertaining to the human person (*LE* IV, 16; 39ff.).[5] And in *Centesimus Annus* he reaffirms the equally traditional right to a just wage (*CA* I, 8; 19).[6] All of these rights stem from the dignity of work, both in its form as labor and as entrepreneurial activity. In *Sollicitudo Rei Socialis* John Paul upholds the right of economic initiative as well within the whole ambit of human rights (*SRS* III, 15; 25–26).[7]

---

serves the older meaning of the term with its stress upon obligation-in-law and with the insistence upon a correlative responsibility. The German term *Recht* is close to the sense of *jus,* and is often translated into English as "right and law." The current English usage, on the other hand, with its emphasis upon a claim inhering in the person as such, does not quite express this social, communal, and objective aspect, but tends to put the individual claim over against an at least hypothetical challenge from another, either an institution or an individual. While the older usage of *jus* is most certainly still operative in John Paul's papal writings, it is true that a new recognition of the subjective aspect and a new emphasis upon the personal is clearly intended.

3. *de modo loquendi:* cf. chap. 4, n. 31.

4. *Laborem Exercens* (*Acta Apostolicae Sedis,* Vatican, vol. 73, 1981, p. 613; hereafter *AAS* vol., yr., p.): ius privati dominii, quatenus iuri usus communis.

5. *AAS* 73, 1981, 618: Haec autem iura sunt intra ipsam summam totam hominis iurium investiganda. . . . Iura enim humana ex labore profecta ingrediuntur ipsum latiorem ambitum eorundem iurium personae principalium.

6. *AAS* 83, 1991, 802: Ius quidem agitur 'salarii iusti.'

7. *AAS* 80, 1988, 529: inter alia iura etiam ius ad propria incepta oeconomica.

These and other rights, he reminds us, have their source in the human person; they stem from the dignity of the human person, and precisely from the person as the subject of work. More than that, those who work for justice are part of what he calls elsewhere "a great movement for the defence of the human person" (CA 3; 10). He speaks of the right of association inherent in individuals, families and other institutions, a right they hold prior to and distinct from their incorporation into a political state (CA I, 11; 24).[8] In the apostolic exhortation *Familiaris Consortio/The Role of the Christian Family in the Modern World* (1981), he upholds the rights of children and the elderly (FC III, 26; 43f. Also, FC III, 27; 45).[9] He speaks there, too, of the irreplaceable and inalienable right of the parents to educate their children (FC III, ii, 2, 36; 59), and of the right of association among families (FC III, ii, 2, 40; 64).

In the apostolic exhortation *Christifideles Laici/The Lay Members of Christ's Faithful People* (1988), he reaffirms a list of rights: "the right to life and to integrity; the right to a house and to work; the right to a family and responsible parenthood; the right to participation in public and political life; the right to freedom of conscience and the practice of religion" (CL 5; 18. Also CL III, 38; 94).[10] Most important of all, then, is the right that comes to each person simply by virtue of his or her humanity, the human right

---

John Paul goes on to say that it is not a matter of economics alone, but also of culture, politics, and of what is simply human: non oeconomica modo est, verum culturalis etiam, politica ac simpliciter humana. One of his first acts as pope was to establish the Concilium pro cultura.

8. The translation renders *consociationes* as "intermediary groups" (AAS 83, 1991, 806).

9. Hereafter, FC. AAS 74, 1982, 111–13. The term "rights" is not actually used of the elderly, but the intent is clear. For the Latin of the next two citations, see AAS 74, 1982, 126–32.

10. Hereafter, CL. CL 5; 18 (AAS 81, 1989, 401): "ius ad vitam et ad integritatem, ius ad dominum et ad laborem, ius ad familiam et ad responsabilem procreationem, ius ad participandam vitam publicam et politicam, ius ad libertatem conscientiae et ad fidem religiosam profitendam." And at CL III, 38; 94 (AAS 81, 1989, 463), warning against the illusory pursuit of rights if the basic right to life is forfeit: "circa humana iura, sicut, exempli gratia, circa ius ad sanitatem, ad domum, ad laborem, ad familiam et ad culturam, nisi maxima vi ius ad vitam, ut primarium ac fontanum, atque ut ceterorum personae iurium condicio, defendatur. . . . Huius iuris subiectum est creatura humana in quolibet sui processus tempore, a conceptione usque ad naturalem mortem."

par excellence: "There exist rights which do not correspond to any work [a human being performs], but which flow from his essential dignity as a person" (*CA* I, 11; 24).[11] This, then, is the human right *formalissime*. It is inherent in each human person by virtue of his rational nature and the image of God carried within. In his vigorous use of the term "right" John Paul does not alter doctrine, but he deepens it by drawing attention to the personal and subjective dimension of the human situation.

To be sure, in harmony with the constant teaching of the Church, and in accord with his own realism of values—grounded in the oft-repeated convertibility of being, truth, and the good— John Paul never separates rights from corresponding obligations.[12] Indeed, even in extolling God's mercy, he is careful not to ignore the conditions of God's justice. While divine mercy "is not just a case of fulfilling a commandment or an obligation of an ethical nature" (*DM* II, 3; 12), neither does authentic forgiveness "cancel out the objective requirements of justice" (*DM* VII, 13; 45).

In using the concept of rights in such extensive and bold ways, John Paul is nonetheless able to remain faithful to the substance of traditional Catholic teaching, just because he underscores the requirement of truthfulness. As we have seen in *The Acting Person* and elsewhere, truthfulness is practical truth acting as the "normogenic" source of the obligation experienced through the conscience of the moral agent.[13] And practical truthfulness is grounded in the convertibility of being, truth and the good, a convertibility confirmed by traditional metaphysics. But, in addition, Wojtyła's phenomenological emphasis upon the ordinary lived ex-

11. *AAS* 83, 1991, 807: "Re quidem vera, ea extra iura quae opere sibi suo homo adipiscitur, alia inveniuntur pariter iura quae nulli ab homine peracto respondent operi sed quae ipsius veluti personae ex essentia ipsa profluunt." John Paul grounds this human right par excellence in the revelation (Gen. 1:26) already remarked upon in *Original Unity*, namely, that man alone has been created *propter seipsam*.

12. Indeed, he even introduces and gives an extended discussion of the controversial notion of the "indirect employer" and the qualified obligation of such an employer to be concerned with the welfare of the workers associated even indirectly with that enterprise (*LE* IV, 16–19; 40–48). The extension of the scope of the obligation is not surprising, given the discussion of "who is my neighbour?" in chapter 7 of *The Acting Person*, and in the supplementary essay to that work (see n. 1 above).

13. See above, chap. III (*AP* 311, n. 52).

perience of the concrete acting person, upon the experience of one's efficacy and responsibility as an agent, in John Paul's writings gives a special authority to the concept of rights.

In keeping with his emphasis on rights properly understood, there is a less noticed but even more fundamental emphasis in his use of the term "subjectivity" and its allied forms. We have already seen the dramatist's attention to and the philosopher's development of the experience of inwardness. That emphasis, so concentrated in Wojtyła's dramas of the living word and driven home by his phenomenological analysis of reflexive consciousness, is continued in the writings of John Paul II. To be sure, an emphasis upon the inner life is no stranger to Christian spirituality, and Karol Wojtyła the philosopher, as well as John Paul II the pope, fully embraces that traditional immanence of the human spirit. What is distinctive about the author, however, is his refashioning of the modern conceptions of experience, inwardness and subjectivity, even while he also draws upon the traditional metaphysics of *suppositum*.

It is not as though experience has not been consulted from the dawning of human consciousness. Even the metaphysician, supposedly the most abstract of minds, nonetheless consults it. How could he not? The difference, however, does not lie in the fact that experience is consulted, but rather in how that consultation takes place. Indeed, the phenomenologist Husserl always attended to the how (*Wie*). And so, it is a matter of two different approaches to experience. The metaphysician consults experience as offering him evidence from which he can reason and infer. He then resolves the evidence into principles and causes which provide an explanation of the evidence. I have tried to show that Wojtyła accepts such reasoning from evidence as essential, even if not wholly adequate, to an integral account of ethical action.[14] But not just any metaphysics will do. Again and again, he insists that an existential metaphysics of actual being (*esse actu*) is required to situate the moral agent in the actual context in which one acts. For such a

14. See the exposition of the *Lubliner Vorlesungen* in chap. 2, above.

metaphysics orients the analysis towards concrete actuality and grounds it in that actuality.

Having secured a realist basis for the whole acting person, Wojtyła *qua* phenomenological realist goes on to consult experience from within, in order to take its measure in its own terms and not only according to its evidential value. Wojtyła's consultation means to dwell within the actual subjective existence of that lived and living experience. Insofar as he employs a phenomenological consultation, then, Wojtyła does not approach experience merely evidentially. By "approaching experience evidentially" I mean: approaching it for the sake of its capacity to offer evidence for the formation of explanatory concepts. Among the sciences and disciplines, insofar as metaphysics comes into play, the context it provides is in a sense indifferent in its terms to all but the universal features of being, for, unlike the special and more restricted sciences, metaphysics is, after all, the comprehensive science of being *qua* being.[15]

The phenomenologist, on the other hand, consults experience in order to release concepts within experience as lived, as felt, as sensed. And so, the phenomenologist Wojtyła consults the living act of thoughtful experiential activity itself, in its own character expressed in its own terms and not in terms of all being. The concepts arrived at experientially must keep an intimate relationship with experience, and must be more descriptive than explanatory, at least inasmuch as explanation is made in terms of more general principles, principles that hold for all being, for *ens inquantum ens*.[16] Thus, for example, in Wojtyła's phenomenology the concept of lived causation is not formed by the observation of various cau-

15. This seems to be the view of Wojtyła, who regards metaphysics as an explanatory science. His principal interest in traditional metaphysics is, of course, in the role that it can play in the analysis of the moral act. My own interest in metaphysics itself leads me to take it to be all that and more, at once abstract and concrete; but this is not the occasion for developing my own view of metaphysics. It is enough that Wojtyła has grasped the substance of traditional metaphysics and put it to work concretely in his own enterprise.

16. Once again, to the best of my knowledge, the foregoing fairly represents Karol Wojtyła's understanding of metaphysics as the universal (and explanatory) science of all being.

sative acts performed by oneself and other beings within the overall context of being. The concept of lived causation is formed phenomenologically within the actual living experience of one's own personal agency and takes shape as the concrete double task of personal integration and transcendence. Such an analysis must address each person's concrete experience of their own agency. And this personal character gives to the analysis an intimacy that observation cannot and should not be expected to give.

This sense of inwardness and intimacy is a striking feature of the work of Karol Wojtyła and John Paul II. We have already seen this sensibility in detail and depth in *The Acting Person*. In *Redemptor Hominis*, John Paul tells us that, in its "utterly new" self-consciousness, the Church, while it assuredly takes revelation as its supreme guide, must also take into account "the premisses given by man's own experience," along with "his reason, and his sense of human dignity" (*RH* III, 17; 38). Great emphasis is laid upon the interiority of the work of the Holy Spirit, which in the words of St. Augustine is "closer than my inmost being" (*DV* II, ii, 54; 92).[17] We are told that, while the journey of the pilgrim Church certainly has an external character, "the essential character of her pilgrimage is interior" (*RMa* II, 1, 25; 37).

Now, the character of this intimacy and interiority is not to be understood in any merely isolated sense. The accent upon intimacy and interiority is not meant to lead to a cul de sac. The intimacy and interiority are expansive. Thus, both the Holy Spirit and Mary, by virtue of the very intimacy associated with them, are said to expand the outreach of human life. Speaking metaphorically in *Dominum et Vivificantem*, John Paul remarks that "In the communion of grace with the Trinity, man's 'living area' is broadened and lifted up to the supernatural level of divine life" (*DV* II, 4, 59; 103–4). And in the intimacy of Mary's faith "first at the Annunciation and then fully at the foot of the Cross, an *interior space*

17. *Dominum et vivificantem: On the Holy Spirit in the Life of the Church and the World* (1986), Vatican translation (Boston: St. Paul Books and Media). The next reference is to *Redemptoris mater: Mother of the Redeemer* (1987), Vatican translation (Boston: St. Paul Books and Media).

was opened up within humanity which the eternal Father can fill 'with every spiritual blessing'" *(RMa* II, 1, 28; 43).[18]

In *Dives in Misericordia,* referring to the dialogue of Israel with God, what strikes John Paul is the people's "special experience of the mercy of God," an experience that formed "the content of intimacy with their Lord" *(DM* III, 3; 14–16).[19] Commenting on the parable of the Prodigal Son, John Paul remarks that heartfelt joy arises in the father because "a fundamental good has been saved: the good of his son's humanity. Although the son has squandered the inheritance, *nevertheless his humanity is saved."* The divine Father draws the measure of His mercy to us from His fidelity to Himself; and by analogy, in the parable "the father's fidelity to himself [*qua* father] is totally concentrated upon the humanity of the lost son, upon his dignity." Such love, John Paul tells us, "springs from the very essence of fatherhood." And the mercy shown by the father in the parable is "the interior form of love that in the New Testament is called *agapē"* *(DM* IV, 6; 21–22). We have already met with that interiority of love in the dramas, and explicitly in *Radiation of Fatherhood.*

The imagery and metaphor prevalent in John Paul's writings are mostly drawn from the Christian tradition, whereas Karol Wojtyła's theatrical images are often unprecedented. But in both, the deliberate, even methodical, conflation of imagery and metaphor with conceptual interpretation is meant to draw out the inner character of that lived experience which is part of the "utterly new" self-consciousness now in possession of the Church. I have already mentioned a shift of consciousness, a new mind-set, that characterizes what is now more and more being called "modernity." This shift in consciousness has implications for everything that engages human life, and specifically for a somewhat new sense of interiority. And so, the shift needs to be brought under the critical eye of both the philosopher and the theologian.

Because I take this shift to be central to the project of Karol

18. We are told further that cultic praise for Mary's faith can lead the Church to "breathe more fully with her 'two lungs,' the East and the West" *(RMa* II, 2, 34; 48).
19. The long note 52 on mercy in the Old Testament should not be overlooked.

Wojtyła/John Paul II, it will be useful to present at some length the description that Karol Wojtyła gave of this shift in 1976:

Since the time of Descartes consciousness has been absolutized, as is reflected in our times in phenomenology through Husserl. In philosophy the gnoseological attitude has superseded the metaphysical; being is constituted in, and to a certain degree through, consciousness. Especially, the reality of the person demands a return to the concept of conscious *being*. This being is not constituted in and by consciousness; quite the contrary, it constitutes both consciousness and the reality of human action as conscious. The person and act, that is, my own self existing and acting, is constituted in consciousness which consequently reflects the existence and action of the self. Thus, one's experience, especially that of one's own self, indicates that consciousness is always rooted in the human subject. Consciousness is not an independent subject, although by a process of exclusion, which in Husserl's terminology is called *epochē*, it may be treated as if it were a subject. This manner of treating consciousness is at the base of the whole so-called "transcendental philosophy." This examines acts of cognition as intentional acts of consciousness directed to trans-subjective matter and, therefore, to what is objective or to phenomena. As long as this type of analysis of consciousness possesses the character of a cognitive method, it can and does bear excellent fruit [by providing descriptions of intentional objects]. However, the method should not be considered to be a philosophy of reality itself. Above all it should not be considered a philosophy of the reality of man or of the human person, since the basis of this method consists in the exclusion (*epochē*) of consciousness from reality or from actually existing being. Despite this, it is undoubtedly necessary to make wider use of this method in the philosophy of man. Consciousness is not an independent subject, but is central for understanding personal subjectivity.[20]

This capital text contrasts the role of being in traditional metaphysics with the role of consciousness in the predominant versions of modern thought, and it succinctly makes three points: it states and describes the shift characteristic of modernity; it is critical of it; but it advocates greater use of its positive aspects.

༄

Let me set forth what I understand this shift to be, in terms that are compatible with those of Karol Wojtyła/John Paul II, though

20. "Person: Subject and Community," *Review of Metaphysics* 33:2 (Dec. 1979): 278 [cf. Grondelski, item 53].

not in his words. The purpose is to provide a broader context that will shed further light upon his understanding of the shift as well as upon my own understanding of his view. I take the term "subject," understood in the modern sense of "subjectivity," to be a form of modern inwardness; that is, I take the modern sense of the term "subject" to be: "subject of thought, feeling, willing, etc." This modern sense of "subject" stands in contrast to the term "subject" understood by traditional metaphysics; for traditional metaphysics understands the term "subject" to mean: "subject of being" (*suppositum*).

Now, "subject" in the modern sense of "subjectivity" was born of the process of modernization itself. Around the sixteenth century, nature came to be viewed more and more externally as an object set over against the mind, and scientific inquiry posited the ideal of a neutered objectivity. There can be no doubt that the nominalism of the late medieval period helped to shape the background to this shift, while the shift itself occurred under the hegemony of the science of mechanics, or rather of the philosophy of mechanism extrapolated from mechanics. No doubt, deeper and broader factors were at work as well, including social factors. It is well known that leading thinkers in the sixteenth and subsequent century launched a sustained attack upon scholastic metaphysics, and particularly upon final causality and the web of ancient metaphysical principles.[21] The whole building of medieval scholasticism was dismantled, leaving only its ruins. What is not so easily recognized is that the principal victim of that attack was not just the lumber of the scholastic framework (the causes), but the resident *being* that lived within the house. For traditional metaphysics claimed for each and every being (and not just for spiritual or mental being) an ontological interiority and depth. This ontological interiority and depth was understood to be brought about by the principles and causes that constituted each being. For each

21. For a further development of the contrast between principles and elements, see K. L. Schmitz, "Analysis by Principles and Analysis by Elements," in *Graceful Reason: Essays in Ancient and Mediaeval Philosophy Presented to Joseph Owens, CSSR*, ed. L. Gerson (Toronto: Pontifical Institute of Mediaeval Studies, 1983), pp. 315–30.

being contained within it: its intrinsic formal and/or material principles, its essential and existential constitutive principles, its finality, and the primordial Presence that remained in communicative continuity with each and every being. Indeed, each and every being was thought to be constituted by the intrinsic principles that flow from the originating creative communication of the manifest-yet-hidden God. In *Radiation of Fatherhood* that communicative presence was dramatically presented as the creative fissure that so troubled Adam.

With the rejection of the scholastic principles, however, the interiority common to all being did not simply disappear; interiority took refuge in the human subject and in the form of human subjectivity. The interiority of being, already recognized and present in traditional metaphysics, came to be excluded from the external world, which was then handed over to the ideal of a neutered objectivity. To repeat: More than final causality and metaphysical principles were thrown out by the leading thinkers of the sixteenth and seventeenth centuries; the interior and ultimately mysterious depth claimed for the internal constitution of every being *qua* being was also dismissed along with those constitutive principles. The short gain was in precision. But the human interiority, the human subject now understood as subjectivity, was turned back upon itself. Descartes's inward journey to the *ego cogito* has served as the most famous and influential emblem of this introspective turn, just because he so clearly wrote the conceptual signature of modernity. It is not surprising, then, that so many postmodern critics of modernity begin with a critique of Descartes.

Many consequences followed from the reign of mechanism and the turn to introspection. One of the most obvious was the definitive status given to a distinction that had been present in a less prominent way among some ancient schools of thought: the distinction between primary and secondary qualities. Objective status was given to primary qualities (dimensionality, size, etc.) and objective status was denied to secondary qualities (color, sound, etc.). The distinction may have begun among scientific enquirers as a methodological principle which permitted the clearing of the ground in favor of measurable quantities; but among philosophers and much of the educated public it quickly turned ontological. That is, the primacy given to the primary qualities seems to have been taken up initially in order to read nature more precisely and efficiently, in the hope that an increase in the knowledge of the forces of nature would bring with it utility and prosperity for mankind.[22] The very success of the distinction so understood, however, led to the conviction that not only was nature susceptible of being *read* in that way, but nature itself is *made up* after the manner of a machine. It has been remarked that, as a result, all that was most familiar to the human being, most immediate and vital—the sensations of color and sound, of taste and smell, the vital indicators of our visible world—were pushed out of the really real into a never-never land. Thus, Descartes considered the sensory percepts and images to be an obscure sort of disturbance at the edges of the human mind; even the empiricists thought of them as wholly subjective.

Except for the modern materialists, who conceded all to matter, what was paramount for others was the fact that conscious interiority was not and could not be reduced to the status of a property of matter.[23] The search for ultimate particles fueled the sciences along the path of classical physics and chemistry. Such reductive analysis could certainly resolve an exterior into a sort of interior, but the resultant interior turned out to consist only of smaller exteriors. A compound was resolved into its elements, and a system was reduced to its particular forces. Reality was handed over to a

22. This is the stated goal of many seventeenth-century thinkers, including Descartes (Letter to Abbé Picot), Francis Bacon (*Novum Organum*), and Hobbes (*De Corpore* I). St. Thomas, too, thought that all study, even metaphysics, has as its purpose the increase of human happiness (*Proemium* to *Commentary on the Metaphysics of Aristotle*), but the emphasis among the modern thinkers is on material productivity rather than upon spiritual or intellectual actuality.

23. We are here at the birth of the modern form of the mind-body problem. A more recent version of that problem speaks of "two languages," the physical and the mental.—As to the concept of matter operative in classical modern materialism (d'Holbach, de la Mettrie, and others), even it was constructed on the basis of the primacy of consciousness.

predefined exteriority, even as subjectivity *qua* human implicitly set the criteria for what was to be considered real.[24]

By turning inward, then, the human subject turned toward itself, in order to establish itself as the basic resting and testing point from which all reality and worth is to be measured. Human consciousness pronounced itself to be *subjectum fundamentum inconcussum* and the guarantor of certitude. As the fundamental and unshakable basis and center of all meaning, value, and reality, the self assumed the role of issuing credit to reality, and it issued that credit in the currency of its own experience. In this modern sense, experience rose to the status of the privileged medium of exchange within the reign of consciousness. It became the "dollar" into which everything could be converted in the sphere of meaning and value. Or, to change the metaphor, it appointed itself to a sort of judicial bench with the power to determine what is to be admitted for further serious consideration. And so, knowledge was converted into meaning, the good into value, and reality into objectivity.[25]

This is the critical nexus of the shift to modernity, for we are at the real birth (if not the initial conception) of the modern sense of experience and of its absolute primacy. It is here that experience in the traditional evidential sense of "acquaintance with" (conveyed by the term *empeiría*) gives way to the term "experience"

24. It is possible to see here a contrast between modern ontology (which, in accord with the modern subject-object distinction and the primacy of the subject, co-opts the object in favor of the interests of the human subject) and traditional metaphysics (as a science of being which transcends the subject-object distinction by virtue of its comprehensive interest in being *qua* being, and ultimately in God as pure being in the sense of *Ipsum Esse*).

25. The classical statement of this "Copernican" turn is to be found in Immanuel Kant's second preface to the *Critique of Pure Reason*: human reason must not be kept in the leading-strings of nature, accepting everything that nature puts before it; rather, nature must be constrained to give answers to questions of reason's own determining, much as an accused is required to answer a judge. In the practical order, the subjective bias of modern liberalism is also to be found in this same priority of subjectivity over the non-subjective; but in the case of liberalism, what is stressed is not specifically subjectivity as theoretical judge, but rather subjectivity as freedom of choice or as *conatus*. (Cf. K. L. Schmitz, "Is Liberalism Good Enough?" in *Liberalism and the Good,* ed. R. Bruce Douglass et al. (New York/London: Routledge, 1990), pp. 86–104.)

in the modern sense. Fortified with the medium of experience, an absolutized consciousness now takes to the field of nature and to the external world in order to impose its own order and values on everything external to consciousness and to translate everything countable into its coin.[26] If the foregoing is true, then the shift to objectivity consists in the displacement of consciousness by one of its own strategies. But this strategy of self-displacement nevertheless places itself at the center; and the self-displacement takes place in the very process by which consciousness drains the external world of all interiority, the "better" to understand and control it. At the level of perception, secondary qualities are made to retreat from the field, surrendering the constitution of objective reality exclusively to the primary qualities of measurable external relations. At the level of concepts, the philosophy of mechanism is left to define the limits and the character of the objectively real.

Whereas at first blush it seemed that consciousness had been driven from the objectively real world, the world of objects, in fact it had simply retreated into its own stronghold in order to co-opt the world of external objects through its demands for precision and for mathematically determinable external relations. This strategy proceeded from a consciousness that had already absolutized itself, implicitly if not explicitly. This, then, is the genesis of the modern sense of subject as subjectivity. We might say that subjectivity is the self-defense by which consciousness fends off a world either hostile to its inhabitation or at least without companionate room for it, even while consciousness subverts the in-

26. An early indication of this imposition is expressed by Descartes in *Discourse on Method*, Part II, Rule 3; but see also the very structure of the a priori in Kant's *Critique of Pure Reason*. The term "imposition" is not quite adequate, since the modern empowerment of subjectivity is not directly a physical force or even a metaphysical empowerment; the strength of its claim lies in epistemology. It is an authoritative power, the exclusive power of setting up the criteria and rules of what will "count" in experience, of what will be taken seriously and further used in the development of knowledge. Nonetheless, the effect of its authority is to resolve all exteriority into what counts for human subjectivity. It might be objected: but what else can perform such a task: To which it may be replied: the issue is not whether human subjectivity must in the end acknowledge what will count for it, but rather whether human subjectivity acknowledges itself or something other (being, God, cosmic fate, etc.) as setting what counts.

tegrity of that world by its imperious demands.[27] The modern shift gave to the human subject an absolute status precisely in its character *qua* consciousness; for human consciousness not only set its own terms but the terms for reality itself. This self-absolutism of modern consciousness leads Wojtyła to renounce intentionality as the hallmark of consciousness and to see in the primacy of intentionality the co-option of the world by idealism.

Now, the interiority of modern subjectivity is vastly different in character and motive from the ontological interiority that, as traditional metaphysics appreciates, is resident in all being as the heritage of every created being. For the causes and principles that constitute created being provide that being with an ultimately inexhaustible depth and mysterious interiority that is partly its own but that also proceeds from and leads back to its creative Source. It is my own understanding that a metaphysics of existential act calls for an ontological depth in all beings, a depth that might well be called "interiority." As metaphysical interiority it is the quite general causative condition of every created being. It seems to me that such a universal ontological interiority is at least implicit in the whole train of Wojtyła's thought from the dramas through the papal writings. Moreover, familiar as he is with the Lublin school and its emphasis upon the concrete, Wojtyła clearly insists upon the concrete nature of that *esse actu* which draws him to St. Thomas's metaphysics. To develop the more radically concrete side of metaphysics even further, the notion of participation (appreciated by Wojtyła in the *Lublin Lectures*) could be developed along the lines it has in the classical studies of St. Thomas by Geiger, Fabro, and others. The development might begin with those texts in St. Thomas that describe *esse* not only as most universal, but also as most intimate (*intimius*). Such a development, it seems to me, is not incompatible with Wojtyła's project, pro-

27. A thorough analysis of my contention would require a discussion of the internal conflict within modern consciousness itself that is implied by my argument. I would take the conflict to be in part due to the strategy by which modern consciousness raises certain partial and more immediate values (precision, certitude, productivity) to the status of primary and comprehensive values. This implies, too, a definite view of the end or perfection of human life and of the values of time.

vided it keeps its focus on the analysis of human action.[28] At any rate, Wojtyła has grasped the universal context of metaphysics and its account of action in terms of ontological principles and causes and has directed that metaphysics towards the concrete human person. For he has not only caught the interior drama of our liberty in his phenomenological analysis as well as in the dramas, he has also underscored the personal dimension within the metaphysics of natural law.

But, if the interiority of modern subjectivity is different in character and motive from that of the ontological interiority of the *suppositum* of traditional metaphysics, so too is modern interiority different from that religious interiority which has from ancient times continued to animate the life of Christian prayer, meditation, contemplation and reflection. For the Christian journey inward is taken for the sake of a salvation that exceeds the self's grasp. Moreover, Christian interiority begins not so much with flight from the world as it does with self-examination, self-purgation and self-denial. For by this *ascesis* it prepares—not to find in itself a refuge (whether Cartesian, Humean or Kantian, rationalist, empiricist or transcendental)—but to place itself before the transcendent Source of whatever being, meaning, and value the human person possesses as a gift received.

In the light of my own understanding of the modern shift as I have just set it forth, Karol Wojtyła/John Paul II has identified the pivotal point in that shift. It is the claim to absolutism on the part of modern human consciousness. Nevertheless, he has sought to turn the modern experience of subjectivity and interiority to whatever good account is to its credit. What is more, he is convinced that in its emphasis on experience, modernity does have some

28. Once again, this is not the place for such a discussion; nor is it likely that Wojtyła had in mind such a development when he called for further development of the line of thought initiated by *Osoba i czyn*. It is my sense that he had in mind a further development of the phenomenological side of the analysis rather than the metaphysical side. One thinks of the phenomenology of the person in Gabriel Marcel's philosophy of the concrete; but one thinks also of Josef de Finance's *Etre et âgir*.—The more general move toward the concrete in Thomistic studies is manifold, in the work of Josef Pieper, Thomas Gilby, and many others.

credit, though not in the exaggerated amount claimed for it by modern philosophers of consciousness. They have set it up as the bank which underwrites the value of all currency, sets the terms for all that is to be accredited, and claims the right to discount what does not fall within those terms. Once consciousness receives a realistic modification after the manner of Wojtyła's project, however, the proper status and role of consciousness within the whole human person can be recognized. We have seen that Wojtyła performs the needed modification by relativizing consciousness. That is, he takes consciousness as an aspect, and with the help of a metaphysics of existential act he restores it to its role within the whole human person. The moral agent, then, is the whole human person as *suppositum*, who is situated within the community of persons and within the universal community of being. Once this is accomplished, the new sense of interiority, which originated in the beleaguered state of modern consciousness (interiority as human subjectivity) can be brought to the service of a realist philosophy of the human person, and through that to the service of Christ who fully reveals man to himself. This modified and combined sense of metaphysical and phenomenological interiority is, it seems to me, the very concept of spirit that the modern world stands in need of, and that Hegel so brilliantly tried but failed to supply.

The question remains, however—and it is our last question—whether such a relativization is possible; for if it is not, it is difficult to see how Wojtyła's full project can be saved from shipwreck. Put more precisely, we should ask whether Wojtyła's phenomenological analysis of interiority is compatible with the realist metaphysics to which he clearly wants to subscribe. It seems to me that it is, under certain conditions.

Before taking up those conditions, let me sound a general note of caution. If we are warned against absolutizing subjective consciousness, we must be wary also lest we over-objectify traditional (pre-modern) metaphysics. Some form of objectification has been around since the discovery of philosophical, mathematical, historical and grammatical discourse among the ancient Greeks; for they objectified the subject-matter of being, number, events and language in order to realize the disciplines of philosophy, mathematics, history and grammar. But such objectification in no way excluded the interior dimension of reality recognized by traditional metaphysics; on the contrary, it gave rise to the philosophy of being.[29] In patristic and medieval thought the theological insights originating from the revelation of the inner life of the Trinity deepened the sense of interiority. For according to both traditional metaphysics and traditional theology, every being in a created universe is signed by God and, in however small a degree, participates in His interiority; each has an "inside." Moreover, it is not just a physical inside such as is disclosed by the breaking open of a rock or a flower, but an ontological inside, the convergence of its parts upon itself. And indeed, the metaphysics of being recognizes the fact that unity is inherently inward seeking: *unum ens indivisum*.[30]

The issue may be addressed in terms of the relation between metaphysical *suppositum* with its ontological interiority and phenomenological subjectivity in its realist form. Karol Wojtyła finds in traditional metaphysics, with its notion of *suppositum entis* and its causal analysis of activity as *influxus entis,* the realistic basis for his phenomenological analysis of human action. In many places John Paul II takes up themes that, while they are enunciated in contemporary terms, are congenial to traditional metaphysics: for example, the distinction between "being" and "having" (*CA* IV, 36; 68), and his criticism of the primacy of things over persons

29. It is interesting in this regard to recall St. Thomas Aquinas's doctrine (in his *Commentary on the De Trinitate of Boethius,* q. 5, a. 1c) that the object of a speculative power, i.e., of theoretical science as the science of things not made or done by us, itself possesses the character of immaterial being. And I would add: of a specific kind of immanence and hence of a specific kind of interiority; in his terms, "the being of intellect." It is for this reason that such an object does not "get in the way," and can serve not as the terminus of the mind but as that through which (*medium quo*) the mind knows the thing. On the other hand, Thomas rejects the notion of theoretical science as a "work of reason," restricting that term to the liberal arts (ad 3).

30. However much one may disagree with some of his formulations, which (especially in *The Phenomenon of Man*) have a predominantly modern (almost Leibnizean) flavor, surely Teilhard de Chardin was possessed of and moved by this great insight.

(*DM* VI, 11; 34).[31] The distinction and the criticism contribute to a new sense of the concrete, which is no longer understood as the complex convergence of abstract principles (concretion) but as the actual existence of a unique individual.

On the other hand, Karol Wojtyła/John Paul II is also seized with a properly modern sense of interiority, experience, and subjectivity. This sensitivity drew him to phenomenology, where he found a recognition of the subjective aspects of human life, and this sensitivity gives to his approach its characteristic emphasis. Thus, John Paul appropriates the language of subjectivity. He speaks of the Church of the Apostles as a collegial subject (*RMi* VI, 61; 90).[32] He tells us further, that the Church is "the social subject of responsibility for divine truth" (*RH* III, 19; 43). He speaks of society, too, in terms of subjectivity. Against the utter objectivism of Socialist Realism, John Paul proclaims the inherent reality and rights of intermediary groups, rights arising out of their subjectivity,

beginning with the family and including economic, political, social and cultural groups which stem from human nature itself and have their own autonomy, always with the view to the common good. This is what I have called the "subjectivity" of society which, together with the subjectivity of the individual, was cancelled out by "Real Socialism." (*CA* II, 13; 28)[33]

Indeed, he adds that "Communist countries were often objects and not subjects" (*CA* III, 28; 51).[34] And when he takes up the topic

31. The theme of "being and having" is associated with the concrete philosophy of Gabriel Marcel, while the criticism of the "primacy of things over persons" is a general theme among the personalists.

32. *AAS* 83, 1991, 309: "'*collegiale subjectum*' *missionis.*" For *RH* (cited next) (*AAS* 71, 1979, 305): *subjectum sociale.*

33. *AAS* 83, 1991, 809–10: "capto a familia initio usque ad oeconomicas et sociales politicas et culturales consociationes quae ex hominis natura orientes— bono communi usque servato—sua ipsorum fruuntur libertate. Id quidem ipsum 'subjectivitatem societatis' vocavimus quae una cum individui subjectivitate a "socialismo reali" deleta est." The quotation marks surrounding "subjectivity of society," along with the personal voice, indicate a consciousness of the novelty of the expression. True subjectivity is opposed to the false "social mechanism or collective subject" that socialism, with its false anthropology, tries to institute.—In *SRS* III, 15; 25–26 (*AAS* 80, 1988, 530), see the term *subiectivo iure,* said of national rights, and the phrase *vera subiectiva proprietas ipsius societatis.*

34. *AAS* 83, 1991, 827: "Nationes olim communistae saepius obiectum fuerunt non subiectum."

THE PROJECT 141

of work in *Laborem Exercens,* as already mentioned, he distinguishes work in the objective, technical and productive sense from
what he calls work in the subjective sense. The subjective dimension of work is not to be measured by productivity; instead, as he
puts it, "The primary basis of the value of work is man himself,"
adding that he means man as the subject of work (*LE* II, 6; 17).[35]
More generally still, he tells us that these rights are meant to secure, not just the rights of the person as worker, but "the creative
subjectivity of the citizen" (*SRS* III, 15; 25–26).[36] And he speaks
out against the abuse of treating human persons simply as market
commodities.[37] He tells us also that the principal abuse against
women is to treat them as objects (*FC* III, i, 24; 41), and he reminds men that the dignity of woman resides in her free subjectivity (*MD* V, 14; 54).[38] Finally, the basis of these rights of
subjectivity is to be found in the dignity of the human person.[39]
It is clear from these uses that John Paul has in mind, not only the
metaphysical sense of subject as *suppositum entis,* but also a cor-

35. *AAS* 73, 1981, 589–90: "*in laborem subiective acceptum* . . . persona, id
est animans subiectivus, capax ad agendum ratione praestituta et rationali, capax
ad deliberandum de se . . . *qualenus est persona, est subiectum laboris,* . . . non
solum ad rationem obiectivam laboris refertur, sed simul nos etiam rationem eius
subiectivam mente comprehendere edocet . . . *primarium fundamentum momenti
laboris esse hominem ipsum,* qui eius est subiectum" (italics in original).
36. *AAS* 80, 1988, 529: "subiectivam videlicet effectricem civis."
37. Cf. *FC* III, 24 (*AAS* 74, 1982, 109–10): "unde homo non persona sed res
existimatur, quasi obiectum emptioni et venditioni."
38. *Mulieris Dignitatem* (*On the Dignity and Vocation of Women*), 1988,
trans. Vatican (Boston: St. Paul Books and Media), "On the basis of the eternal
'unity of the two' [cf. *Original Unity of Man and Woman*], this dignity directly
depends on woman herself, as a subject responsible for herself, and at the same
time it [i.e., the acknowledgement of woman's dignity] is 'given as a task' to man."
AAS 80, 1988, 1687–88: "Ex aeterna 'duorum unitate,' haec dignitas directo ex
ipsa pendet muliere, utpote subiecto per se responsali, simulque 'uti officium' viro
concreditur." In the preceding sentence of the text, "*modo propriam sui naturam*"
is translated as "their own subjectivity," which stretches the Latin but catches its
sense in context.—In the same text he notices that too often in actual fact woman
is treated as an object of desire and exploitation, when in truth she is the co-subject
(*compar subiectum*) of man's existence in the world.—For a discussion of women's
rights, see *MD* 10, 39ff., and throughout.
39. *AAS* 81, 1989, 401: "Ex quo ille sensus dignitatis personalis omnium
hominum semper et amplius diffunditur ac vehementis asserveratur. . . . Nam
'homo' prorsus non est 'res' aut 'obiectum' quo uti possum, sed semper est 'subiectum' conscientia et libertate donatum."

rected modern sense of subject as "subjectivity" in distinction from the modern sense of "object" as "thing lacking interiority."

Now, the concept of *suppositum* or supposit in the metaphysics of being signifies that which is ontologically prior in being to whatever it sustains; it is the privileged center of being, and the ontological basis of each entity. The supposit can be described as substance or concrete essence, or, better yet, as the subject of existential act. It is that which in some primary sense exists in and through itself (*ens per se*). Since, in a metaphysics of existential act, the supposit is the ultimate bearer of reality, and since it has the interiority that is proper to all created being, the human supposit does not stand over against the interiority of the human being as does the sheer externality of an object in the modern sense. On the contrary, in the metaphysics of being the human supposit has not had cast out of it all ontological interiority (along with the causes that ground that interiority). And so, precisely because it is not a reified object in this modern sense, such a metaphysical supposit does not in principle exclude the presence and recognition of a specific sort of interiority within supposits or subjects of the human kind. Human interiority is compatible with such a metaphysics. In addition to its own specific interiority, human subjectivity shares an ontological interiority with all beings.

Nevertheless, as Wojtyła says, in analyzing the human supposit, metaphysics does not exploit human interiority specifically as an aspect of the human person; instead, it identifies that interiority as a mode of being (as rational, intellectual, spiritual being). And so metaphysics does not take up human interiority in its most intimate character; it takes up human interiority in the medium of being but not in the medium of experience. But, it is precisely because the traditional metaphysics of being is pre-modern that it need not reject the light thrown upon human interiority by Wojtyła's phenomenological analysis. It is just because traditional metaphysics does not absorb being into experience that its sense of ontological interiority is compatible with and open to the modern experience of interiority realistically considered. By "premodern" I do not mean "outdated." I mean rather that, just because the traditional metaphysics of being has not suffered the divorce of subjectivity and objectivity in their modern and mutually exclusive senses, such a metaphysics can provide a more adequate base for a modified modern sense of interiority, i.e. for a relativized sense of interiority. Hence, just because traditional metaphysics does not empty nonconscious things of their appropriate interiority and depth, it can find the grounds for an interiority shared in common by conscious and non-conscious beings. Traditional metaphysics of being can then identify the distinctive mode of human interiority in terms of intellectuality and freedom, leaving to a realist phenomenology the description of the experienced inner drama of responsible liberty.

To sum up: I find that the project of the philosopher Wojtyła succeeds, if the following five conditions hold. The first three conditions pertain chiefly to the metaphysics of being, while the last two touch upon phenomenology.

The first condition is that the traditional metaphysics of being as existential act does actually avoid the modern separation of being into subject and object, when that separation is taken as the primary division of reality. For, to accept the primacy of that distinction is to give to human subjectivity a privileged double role: on the one hand, human subjectivity stands over against the object even as, on the other hand, it underwrites the terms that define the purportedly significant features of the object. By contrast, the being considered by traditional metaphysics is both trans-objective and trans-subjective.

The second condition is that each and every being has its own mode of interiority and depth, in that it is constituted through causal participation and by the resonance of shared being within the community of beings. Originally and ultimately, the metaphysical subjectivity (*suppositum*) of each creature is sustained within each creature by its constitutive relation to the divine creator (*esse creaturae adesse Deum*). The subjectivity immanent within every created being is not as such the subjectivity of human consciousness—such a universal ascription ends in idealism, whether it goes by that name or not. In those beings in whom it is appropriate, that is, in human and other intelligent creatures, interiority takes the form of personal immanence, of immaterial and spiritual existence. In its human form the properly human ontological interiority is anthropological subjectivity (*suppositum humanum*).

The third condition is from the side of the account of moral action. If the analyst-as-metaphysician is to service that same analyst-as-phenomenologist, the metaphysician must acknowledge the limits of metaphysical discourse, even as he situates the phenomenological interpretation of interiority within the modes of being specified by metaphysics. That is, as he or she resolves the experience of the human person into terms of immaterial, immanent, spiritual, contingent being, and expresses that experience in accordance with the transcendental features and modes of being, the metaphysician must recognize that his or her concepts only identify subjective interiority within the comprehensive horizon of being as being; they do not move intimately within that subjective interiority in its own terms.[40]

The fourth condition (also from the side of the account given) is that the phenomenology forged in the full account of the human being and of human action is radically realist and without the methodological reservation against existence and causality that prevented the full experience of the moral agent from being acknowledged.[41] This modification of phenomenology is meant to relativize consciousness and to recognize that the primary subject of human being and human action is the whole human person within the context of the community of being. Human consciousness must not be taken to be absolute, but must be understood as relative to the person, whose experienced interiority can, therefore, be interpreted through the bracketing of consciousness as an aspect.

40. Analogously to Maritain's distinction between the practically-practical and the speculatively-practical I am tempted to distinguish metaphysics as "reflectively-reflective" from phenomenology as "immediately-reflective"; but it is late for such subtleties.

41. See Wojtyła's discussion of Scheler's phenomenological reservation (*Vorbehalt*) in *Lubliner Vorlesungen*, pp. 48ff., with supporting citations of contemporary psychologists.

The fifth condition is that, since we are interpreting action, we have every right to consider, not simply the distinction between the methodical disciplines of metaphysics and phenomenology, but more concretely the unitary human person who is both subjectivity and supposit. What is more, as inquirers ourselves we cannot forget that both our descriptions and our explanations terminate in the same unique reality, the concrete person. For experience itself, free of methodological reservations, discloses and warrants the recognition of the whole human person and moral agent as a responsible cause. And so, in the very action of giving his or her account, the phenomenologist must transcend one's own phenomenology, in order to recognize as necessary for the completion of his or her analysis, the human person whom metaphysics identifies as *suppositum*. For the concrete human person is the context within which the descriptions must move, the basis in which they are rooted, and the terminal towards which they are directed. That is, he or she must acknowledge the identity of the phenomenological subjectivity with the metaphysical supposit who is the human person. With that identification the full reality of the person not only is confirmed by metaphysical analysis, but is discovered most intimately through the experienced fact of moral agency. It has also been presented dramatically in the theater of the living word.

These five conditions amount to this: It is in the acting person that the acts of phenomenological interpretation and the acts of metaphysical explanation meet in their concrete and efficacious source. So that by acting, the human person outreaches both explanation and interpretation. For it is the concrete human person who, in acting, takes up the task of integration and transcendence and thereby becomes the human agent who engages with others in the community of being.

∽

With this I bring these reflections to a close. Karol Wojtyła/John Paul II has brought to the office of Peter the experience of student and worker, playwright and poet, philosopher, theologian, and professor in the exercise of his calling as priest and pope. He exhibits a thoroughly contemporary understanding, rooted in a knowledge of the traditions of classical, medieval, and modern thought. That understanding is reflected in writings that range from dramas and poems through philosophical and theological works, to his letters and talks as teacher for the universal Church. He has acted out his conviction on stage and podium, in prayer and before the altar. In a bewildering variety of places he has met with pauper and prince, and people of every sort and condition. This most public of pontiffs, most traveled of popes, has long been the pilgrim of an inner path that has taken him in the midst of others to Christ who is the eternal center of the human drama. "At the still point, there the dance is. . . . And do not call it fixity. Where past and future are gathered. . . . Except for the point, the still point, there would be no dance, and there is only the dance."[42]

42. From T. S. Eliot, *Burnt Norton*.

Appendix
Sources for the Study
of Karol Wojtyła's Thought

JOHN M. GRONDELSKI

Although Pope John Paul II has occupied the Chair of Peter for over a decade, serious academic study of his thought itself (particularly in its pre-pontifical form), as well as its potential for fostering an authentic *aggiornamento* in the contemporary Church and world, remains in its infancy, especially in the English-speaking world. While Karol Wojtyła's books (except for his *habilitacja* dissertation on Scheler) have been translated into English, many of his important articles are available only in other languages such as French, German, and Italian, while some can be found only in their original Polish. There is little systematic study of Wojtyła's thought in most English-speaking universities—for example, the number of doctoral dissertations written on aspects of John Paul's thought in the United States is extremely low. Very few works are available that aim at applying Wojtyła's insights to theological and philosophical enterprises in America. Likewise, very few works in the English-speaking world attempt to build upon and develop the creative insights whose foundations Wojtyła laid in his pre-papal writings. The purpose of this appendix, then, is to facilitate research into Pope John Paul II's pre-papal corpus. It is hoped that end will be achieved in three ways; (i) by noting available resources for study of Wojtyła's thought; (ii) by supplying a select bibliography (Wojtyła's complete pre-papal bibliography exceeds six hundred entries) of some of Wojtyła's most important writings, together with references to some available translations; and (iii) by listing a few of the most important items of secondary literature helpful in a study of this theme.

I. Resource Centers for Study of the Pre-Pontifical Thought of Pope John Paul II

The two leading centers for study of the thought of Karol Wojtyła are in Poland and in Rome. They share a good cooperative relationship. The Instytut Jana Pawła II (John Paul II Institute) was established in June 1982 at Katolicki Uniwersytet Lubelski (KUL—Catholic University of Lublin), which was the only independent university behind the Iron Curtain, where

147

Wojtyła served as a professor in the 1950s. The Institute maintains a collection of works by and about Wojtyła, sponsors academic conferences and symposia on Wojtyła's thought, and publishes a quarterly review, *Ethos*, primarily in Polish. The Rev. Dr. Tadeusz Styczeń (Wojtyła's assistant in the Ethics section) is director; Prof. Dr. Jerzy Gałkowski is vice-director. The Institute can be contacted at Katolicki Uniwersytet Lubelski, Al. Racławickie, 14, Lublin, 20-950, Poland; Telex: 0643235-KUL-PL.

The Fundacja Jana Pawła II (John Paul II Foundation) was established by the Holy See in October 1981 in Rome to promote those values closest to John Paul and his teaching. Its work is carried on by the Polski Instytut Kultury Chrześcijańskiej (Polish Institute of Christian Culture; address: Via di Porta Anjelica, 63, Rome, 00-193, Italy; telephone: 06/6861844), the Ośrodek Dokumentacji Pontyfikatu Jana Pawła II (Center for Documentation of the Pontificate of John Paul II; address: Via Cassia N, 1200, Rome, 00-189, Italy; telephone: 06/3766696), and the Dom Jana Pawła II (John Paul II Home; same address on Via Cassia N.). The Polish Institute of Christian Culture (director: Rev. Dr. Marian Radwan, SCJ) conducts academic research, sponsors symposia, and publishes books. Symposia organized by the Institute, in Rome and in Poland, have treated "Pastoral Implications of John Paul Pilgrimage's to Poland," "The Church and the Christian Peoples of East–Central and Northern Europe," "The Christian Heritage of European Culture in Contemporary Consciousness," "The Gospel and Culture: The Central European Experience," and "The Problem of Man's Liberation." Among the Institute's publications have been: A. Stępień, ed., *Wobec filozofii marksistowskiej: Polskie doświadczenia* [On Marxist Philosophy: The Polish Experience]; T. Styczeń and M. Radwan, eds., *Problem wyzwolenia człowieka* [The Problem of Man's Liberation]; *L'héritage chrétien de la culture européenne dans la conscience des contemporains*, as well as various collections of John Paul's statements and magisterial documents, especially on social teaching and on the relation of faith and culture. The Center for Documentation of the Pontificate of John Paul II (director: Msgr. Dr. Michał Jagosz) serves as an archival center for writings by and about John Paul II both before and after his papal election. It collects copies of books, articles, newspaper writings, recordings, and memorabilia connected with the life, thought, and activities of Pope John Paul II, and gladly welcomes collaboration from anyone who can supply materials for its collections. The John Paul II Home is a house for pilgrims in Rome. The Foundation also sponsors a three-week summer seminar (usually from the last Monday of June to around July 15) in Rome for persons interested in studying Polish culture (literature, art, film, history, theology, etc.), with field trips into Rome and its environs. Undergraduate college credit is available for those interested. The summer session can be contacted at Via di Porta Angelica, 63, Rome, 00-193, Italy.

In the United States, the Pope John Paul II Center was established in 1978 at the Orchard Lake Schools in Michigan. The Schools were

founded in 1885 originally as a seminary for preparing priests for sac-
erdotal service in the Polish community in the United States. Today, they
consist of SS. Cyril and Methodius Seminary, St. Mary's College, and St.
Mary's Preparatory, as well as various centers. Due to their Polish origins,
the Schools had built up a respectable collection of theological books and
journals from Poland (including many in which Wojtyła's publications
originally appeared) which suddenly acquired new value after John Paul's
pontifical election. Cardinal Wojtyła had twice visited the Schools, in
1969 and 1976. The Center publishes a newsletter. The Pope John Paul II
Center can be contacted at The Orchard Lake Schools, Orchard Lake,
Michigan, 48033; telephone: (313) 682-1885.

One institution that has taken a particular interest in the thought of
Karol Wojtyła is the Internationale Akademie für Philosophie im Fürsten-
tum Liechtenstein. The Academy publishes the journal *Aletheia*, in which
studies of John Paul's thought have appeared, and treats Wojtyła's
thought in connection with various courses in its graduate program.
KUL's Father Tadeusz Styczeń has lectured in its program. Prof. Dr. Josef
Seifert is director of the Academy. Address: Obergass 75, FL-9494
Schaan, Liechtenstein; telephone: 075/28675.

II. Select Bibliography of Most Significant Books and Articles by Karol Wojtyła

For a complete bibliography of Karol Wojtyła's pre-papal writings, see
Wiktor Gramatowski and Zofia Wilińska, *Karol Wojtyła w świetle pub-
likacji/Karol Wojtyła negli scritti: Bibliografia* [Karol Wojtyła in the Light
of His Writings: A Bibliography] (Vatican City: Libreria Editrice Vaticana, 1980). The bibliography lists Wojtyła's pre-papal writings by year,
providing the original Polish title and source together with an Italian
translation of the title. The bibliography also lists articles about Karol
Wojtyła written prior to his papal election. In the following list, references
are provided where a translation of the material is available. Where none
is available, a brief synopsis of the work's content is noted. Where no
synopsis is supplied, the article was unavailable to the author at the time
of writing.

A. Abbreviations

E. English
EzL Karol Wojtyła. *Erziehung zur Liebe: Mit einer ethischen
Fibel.* Stuttgart: Seewald Verlag, 1979.
EV Karol Wojtyła. *En Esprit et en Vérité: Recueil de textes
1949–1978.* Trans. Gwendoline Jarczyk. Paris: Le Centurion,
1980.
F. French
Fasc. Fascicle

G.   German
LV   Karol Wojtyła. *Lubliner Vorlesungen*. Stuttgart: Seewald
        Verlag, 1981.
PG   Karol Wojtyła. *Primat des Geistes: Philosophische Schriften*.
        Stuttgart: Seewald Verlag, 1980.
S.   Spanish
VdK   Karol Wojtyła. *Von der Königswürde des Menschen*.
        Stuttgart: Seewald Verlag, 1980.

B. Theological Writings

1. "Apostolstwo swieckich" [The Apostolate of the Laity]. *Ateneum Kapłańskie*, year 60, vol. 71, fasc. 5 (1968): 274–30. Since Vatican II the apostolate of the laity has experienced profound new dimensions. Both on the level of Church teaching (particularly *Gaudium et Spes*, *Lumen Gentium*, and *Apostolicam Actuositatem*) and on the level of Church structures (e.g., Consilium de Laicis) the lay apostolate has been emphasized. The Good Shepherd, being ready to lay down his life for man's dignity, for his immortal soul, provides the model for the apostle. While the lay apostolate takes a variety of shapes, all must lead to Christ "who reveals man to himself," since the lay apostolate should bring man to plumb the meaning of his personal dignity.
2. "Biskup—sługa wiary: Podstawy teologiczne problemu." *Ateneum Kapłańskie*, year 68, vol. 87, fasc. 2 (1976): 223–40. E.: "Bishops as Servants of the Faith," Irish Theological Quarterly 43 (1976), no. 4:260–73. Both texts represent Wojtyła's paper to the European Bishops' Symposium in Rome, October 14–18, 1975.
3. "Chrześcijanin a kultura" [The Christian and Culture]. *Znak* 16 (1964), no. 10:1153–57. F.: "Le chrétien et la culture, *EV*, pp. 187–92. G.: "Der Christ und die Kultur," *VdK*, pp. 79–83.
4. "Człowiek jest osobą (Stosunek Kościoła do świata współczesnego)" [Man Is a Person (The Relation of the Church to the Contemporary World)]. *Tygodnik Powszechny* 18 (1964), no. 52:2. G.: "Der Mensch als Person," *VdK*, pp. 43–47.
5. "Czym powinna być teologia moralna?" [What Should Moral Theology Be?]. *Ateneum Kapłańskie*, year 51, vol. 58, fasc. 1/3 (1959): 97–104. F.: "Ce que doit être la théologie morale?" *EV*, pp. 71–81.
6. "Etyka a teologia moralna" [Ethics and Moral Theology]. *Znak* 19 (1967), no. 9:1077–82. The current situation of moral theology; the place of philosophizing in speculative moral theology; the Kantian problematic of shifting the focus in ethics from *telos* to the grounding of moral norms—challenge for moral theology? moral theology as being renewed through an awareness of the Incarnate God-man Jesus Christ as a living model for man here and now (and not just man's future end) and through a critical appreciation of the turn to the subject found in phenemonological method.

7. *Faith According to St. John of the Cross*. Trans. Jordan Aumann. San Francisco: Ignatius Press, 1981. Translation of Wojtyła's dissertation at the Pontifical University of St. Thomas Aquinas, Rome.

8. "Inspiracja maryjna Vaticanum II" [The Marian Inspiration of Vatican II]. In Bohdan Bejze, ed., *W kierunku prawdy* [In the Direction of the Truth]. Warsaw, 1976, pp. 112–21. The teaching of the Second Vatican Council on Mary, especially on Mary as Mother of the Church.

9. "Komentarz teologiczno-duszpasterski do aktu dokonanego na Jasnej Górze dnia 3 maja 1966" [A Theological-Pastoral Commentary to the Act Carried Out on Jasna Góra May 3, 1966]. *Ateneum Kapłański*, year 64, vol. 79, fasc. 1/2 (1972): 5–21. 1966 marked the millennium of Christianity in Poland. The Polish bishops rededicated the country to Mary, Queen of Poland. The meaning of their act and its roots both in traditional Mariology and contemporary theology are examined in this article.

10. "Notatki na marginesie konstytucji 'Gaudium et Spes'" [Notes on the Margin of the Constitution *Gaudium et Spes*]. *Ateneum Kapłańskie*, year 62, vol. 74, fasc. 1 (1970): 3–6. G.: "Bemerkungen über di Konstitution Gaudium et Spes," *VdK*, pp. 143–46.

11. "Objawienie Trójcy Świętej [sic] a świadomość zbawienia w świetle nauki Vaticanum II" [The Revelation of the Holy Trinity and the Consciousness of Salvation in the Light of the Teaching of Vatican II]. In *Z zagadnień kultury chrześcijańskiej* [On the Matter of a Christian Culture]. Lublin, 1973, pp. 11–19. Represents a treatment similar to the same topic discussed in *Sources of Renewal*.

12. "Perspektywy człowieka—integralny rozwój a eschatologia" [Perspectives of Man: Integral Development and Eschatology]. *Colloquium Salutis* 7 (1975): 133–45. G.: "Die Perspektiven des Menschen," *VdK*, pp. 65–78.

13. "Problematyka dojrzewania człowieka: Aspekt antropologiczno-teologiczny" [The Problem of Man's Maturation: Anthropologico-Theological Aspects]. *Nasza Rodzina* 9 (1977): 2–15.

14. "Rozważanie o śmierci" [Considerations about Death] (Poem). *Znak* 27 (1975), no. 3:271–76. E.: "Meditation on Death," in Wojtyła, *Collected Poems*, trans. Jerzy Peterkiewicz. New York: Random House, 1982, pp. 147–58.

15. "La sainteté sacerdotale comme carte d'identité." *Seminarium*, 30 (1978), no. 1:167–80.

16. "Sobór a praca teologów" [The Council and the Work of Theologians]. *Tygodnik Powszechny* 19 (1965), no. 9:1. F.: "Le concile et le travail des théologiens," *EV*, pp. 227–30.

17. "Sobór od wewnątrz. List do redakcji 'Tygodnika Powszechnego'" [The Council from the Inside: A Letter to the Editor of *Tygodnik Powszechny*]. *Tygodnik Powszechny* 19 (1965), no. 16: 1, 3. F.: "Le concile vu de l'intérieur," *EV*, pp. 231–40.

18. "Świadomość Kościoła wedle Vaticanum II" [The Consciousness of the Church According to Vatican II]. In *W nurcie zagadnień posobo-*

rowych, vol 5: *Jan XXIII i jego dzieło* [In the Current of Post-Conciliar Considerations, vol. 5: John XXIII and His Works]. Ed. Bohdan Bejze. Warsaw, 1972, pp. 255–309. Represents a treatment similar to the same topic discussed in *Sources of Renewal.*

19. "Tajemnica i człowiek" [Mystery and Man]. *Tygodnik Powszechny* 7 (1951), nos. 51/52:1–2. F.: "Le mystère et l'homme," *EV,* pp. 21–28. G.: "Das Geheimnis und der Mensch," *VdK,* pp. 49–57.

20. "Teologia i teologowie w Kościele posoborowym" [Theology and Theologians in the Post-Conciliar Church]. In *Teologia i antropologia* [Theology and Anthropology]. Kraków: Polski Towarzystwo Teologiczne, 1972, pp. 27–42. Vatican II demonstrated in a special way the collaboration of bishops and theologians, a fruitful work that should continue; the task of "reinterpretation," particularly in a personalistic perspective, of theological statements in light of Vatican II, for contemporary man must go on; a method of reinterpretation that, however, ends in putting the essence (not the formulation) of doctrinal teaching into question is to be rejected; some doctrinal deviations among certain theologians might be traced to deficient philosophical perspectives underlying their theological methodology; the contemporary theological scene in Poland is vigorous and productive; fidelity to doctrinal essence is not mere conservatism.

21. "Teologia kapłaństwa" [The Theology of the Priesthood]. *Częstochowskie Studia Teologiczne* 5 (1977): 7–18. The theology of the priesthood in light of the Second Vatican Council; the relationship of creation and Redemption; the mutual ordering of the priesthood of the faithful and of the ministerial priesthood; the priesthood in building up the community of the People of God in the Church.

22. "Teologiczne podstawy duszpasterskiej misji kapłana" [Theological Foundations of the Pastoral Mission of the Priest]. In Józef Majka, ed., *Osobowość kapłańska* [Priestly Personality]. Wrocław, 1976, pp. 55–69. The mission of the priest today; Vatican II on the priest's mission as gathering the family of God, especially in celebration of the Eucharist, and as rearing in the faith, especially in helping each person discern his proper vocation in the *triplex munus Christi;* the Good Shepherd and the priest; the identity of the priest as intrinsically bound up with his sacramental ministry by which, in exercising his vocation, he furthers the good of salvation.

23. *U podstaw odnowy: Studium o realizacji Vaticanum II.* Kraków: Polskie Towarzystwo Teologiczne, 1972. E.: *Sources of Renewal: The Implementation of the Second Vatican Council.* Trans. P. S. Falla. San Francisco: Harper and Row, 1979.

24. "Uniwersytet Katolicki: koncepcja i zadania" [The Catholic University: Concept and Task]. *Zeszyty Naukowe Katolickiego Uniwersytetu Lubelskiego* 11 (1968), nos. 3/4:13–16. Article written to celebrate the fiftieth anniversary of the founding of KUL; "University" as designating a community of scholars and as pointing to the universality of truth amidst a diversity of disciplines; the university as serving man's quest

for truth and as affirming the legitimate autonomy of created reality; the Catholic University as serving that legitimate autonomy and as seeking an integral vision of the human person; the role of the Catholic University in the mission of the Church.

25. "Vaticanum II a praca teologów" [Vatican II and the Work of Theologians]. *Collectanea Theologica* 36 (1966), fasc. 1/4:8–14. G.: "Das II. Vatikanische Konzil und die Arbeit der Theologen," *VdK*, pp. 147–54.

26. "Znaczenie kardynała Stefana Wyszyńskiego dla współczesnego Kościoła" [The Significance of Stefan Cardinal Wyszyński for the Contemporary Church. *Zeszyty Naukowe Katolickiego Uniwersytetu Lubelskiego* 14 (1971), no. 3:19–37.

27. "Znaczeni konstytucji 'Dei Verbum' w teologii" [The Significance of the Constitution "Dei Verbum" in Theology]. In *Idee przewodne soborowej konstytucji o Objawieniu Bożym* [The Central Ideas of the Conciliar Constitution on Divine Revelation]. Kraków, 1969, pp. 7–11. Vatican II's Constitution on Divine Revelation; personalistic emphasis and thrust found in its concept of revelation.

28. "Znaczeni konstytucji pastoralnej dla teologów" [The Significance of the Pastoral Constitution for Theologians]. *Collectanea Theologica* 38 (1968), fasc. 1:5–18.

29. *Znak, któremu sprzeciwiać sie beda.* Poznań: Pallotinum, 1976. E.: *Sign of Contradiction.* Crossroad Books. New York: Seabury Press, 1979.

C. Philosophical Writings

30. "Akt und Erlebnis: Monographische Studie," *LV*, pp. 27–104.

31. "Co to jest asceza?" [What Is Ascetism?]. In the "Elementarz etyczny" series, no. 14. *Tygodnik Powszechny* 11 (1957), no. 40:7. F.: "Qu'est-ce que l'ascèse?" *EV*, pp. 140–41. G.: "Was ist das, Askese?" *EzL*, pp. 120–23.

32. "Etyka niezależna w świetle idei sprawiedliwości" [Independent Ethics in the Light of the Idea of Justice]. In the "Elementarz etyczny" series, no. 20. *Tygodnik Powszechny* 12 (1958), no. 6:7. F.: "Une éthique indépendante à la lumière de l'idée de justice," *EV*, pp. 155–59. G.: "Die unabhängige Ethik im Lichte der Idee der Gerechtigkeit," *EzL*, pp. 147–54.

33. "Ewangeliczna zasada naśladowania: Nauka źródeł Objawienia a system filozoficzny Maxa Schelera" [The Evangelical Principle of Imitation: The Teaching of the Sources of Revelation and the Philosophical System of Max Scheler]. *Ateneum Kapłański*, year 49, vol. 55, fasc. 1 (1957): 57–67. G.: "Das Prinzip der Nachahmung im Evangelium anhand der Quellen der Offenbarung und das philosophische System von Max Scheler," *PG*, pp. 263–80.

34. "Das Gute und der Wert," *LV*, pp. 105–249.

35. "Humanizm a cel człowieka" [Humanism and Man's End]. In the

"Elementarz etyczny" series, no. 8. *Tygodnik Powszechny* 11 (1957), no. 31:7. F.: "Humanisme et fin de l'homme," *EV*, pp. 126–29. G.: "Der Humanismus und das Ziel des Menschen," *EzL*, pp. 98–103.
36. "Idea i pokora" [Idea and Humility]. In the "Elementarz etyczny" series, no. 15. *Tygodnik Powszechny* 11 (1957), no. 41:7. F.: "Idée et humilité," *EV*, pp. 141–44. G.: "Die Idee und die Demut," *EzL*, pp. 124–27.
37. "The Intentional Act and the Human Act, i.e., Act and Experience." *Analecta Husserliana* series, vol. 5. Dodrecht, Holland: D. Reidel, 1976, pp. 269–80.
38. "Kamień węgielny etyki społecznej" [The Cornerstone of Social Ethics]. In the "Elementarz etyczny" series, no. 17. *Tygodnik Powszechny* 12 (1958), no. 1:7. F.: "La pierre angulaire de l'éthique sociale," *EV*, pp. 146–48 (text missing one paragraph at end). G.: "Der Grundstein der sozialen Ethik," *EzL*, pp. 131–36.
39. "Moralność a etyka" [Morality and Ethics]. In the "Elementarz etyczny" series, no. 1. *Tygodnik Powszechny* 11 (1957), no. 9:3. F.: "Morale et éthique," *EV*, pp. 105–7. G.: "Moral und Ethik," *EzL*, pp. 63–66.
40. "Myśli o uczestnictwie" [Thoughts on Participation]. *Znak* 23 (1971), nos. 2/3: 209–25.
41. "Natura i doskonałość" [Nature and Perfection]. In the "Elementarz etyczny" series, no. 5. *Tygodnik Powszechny* 11 (1957), no. 13:11. F.: "Nature et perfection," *EV*, pp. 116–19. G.: "Die Natur und die Vollkommenheit," *EzL*, pp. 81–86.
42. "Natura ludzka jako podstawa formacji etycznej" [Human Nature as the Foundation of Ethical Formation]. *Znak* 11 (1959), no. 6:693–97. F.: "La nature humaine comme base de la formation éthique," *EV*, pp. 82–87.
43. "Norm und Glück" (1956–67 Lectures at KUL). *LV*, pp. 251–414.
44. *Ocena możliwości zbudowania etyki chrześcijańskiej przy założeniach systemu Maksa Schelera* [On the Possibility of Constructing a Christian Ethic on the Basis of the System of Max Scheler]. Lublin: TNKUL, 1959. G.: "Über die Möglichkeit, eine christliche Ethik in Anlehnung an Max Scheler zu schaffen," *PG*, pp. 35–197. S.: *Max Scheler y la ética cristiana.* Madrid: Biblioteca de Autores Cristianos, 1982.
45. "O kierowniczej lub służebnej roli rozumu w etyce: na tle poglądów Tomasza z Akwinu, Hume'a i Kanta" [On the Directive or Serving Role of Reason in Ethics from the Viewpoints of Thomas Aquinas, Hume, and Kant]. *Roczniki Filozoficzne* 6 (1968), fasc. 2:13–31.
46. "O metafizycznej i fenomenologicznej podstawie normy moralnej (w oparciu o koncepcję sw. Tomasza z Akwinu oraz Maksa Schelera) [On the Metaphysical and Phenomenological Foundation of Moral Norms, on the Bases of the Concepts of St. Thomas Aquinas and Max Scheler]. *Roczniki Teŏlogiczno-Kanoniczne* 6 (1959), fasc. 1/2:99–124. G.:

"Über die metaphysische und die phänomenologische Grundlage der moralischen Norm," *PG*, pp. 231–62.

47. "O pochodzeniu norm moralnych" [On the Origin of Moral Norms]. In the "Elementarz etyczny" series, no. 3. *Tygodnik Powszechny* 11 (1957), no. 11:3. F.: "De l'origine des normes morales," *EV*, pp. 111–14. G.: "Über die Herkunft der moralischen Normen," *EzL*, pp. 73–77.

48. *Osoba i czyn* [The Person and the Act]. Kraków: Polskie Towarzystwo Teologiczne, 1969. E.: *The Acting Person*. Trans. Andrzej Potocki. Rev. Anna-Teresa Tymieniecka. In the *Analecta Husserliana* series, vol. 10. Boston/Dodrecht, Holland: D. Reidel, 1979. Various criticisms of the fidelity of this translation have been raised, e.g., Marian Jaworski, et al., "O autentyczny tekst 'Osoby i czynu,'" *Tygodnik Powszechny*, September 26, 1982. This author would also regard this text as at variance with the Polish original. For those who cannot secure access to the original Polish, it might be helpful to compare passages of this English translation with the French and/or German translations of this work when doing research involving this book.

49. "Osoba i czyn na tle dynamizmu człowieka" [The Person and the Act from the Viewpoint of the Dynamism of Man]. In *O Bogu i o człowieku: problemy filozoficzne* [On God and On Man: Philosophical Problems]. Ed. Bohdan Bejze. Warsaw, 1968, pp. 204–26. Represents a treatment similar to the same topic discussed in *The Acting Person*.

50. "Osoba i czyn. Refleksywne funkcjonowanie, świadomości i jej emocjonalizacja" [The Person and the Act: The Reflexive Functioning of Consciousness and Its Emotionalization]. *Studia Theologica Varsuviensia* 6 (1968), no. 1:101–19. Represents a treatment similar to the same topic discussed in *The Acting Person*.

51. "Osoba i czyn w aspekcie świadomości" [The Person and the Act in the Aspect of Consciousness]. In *Pastori et Magistro*. Ed. Andrzej Krupa. Lublin: TNKUL, 1966, pp. 293–305. Represents a treatment similar to the same topic discussed in *The Acting Person*.

52. "Osoba ludzka a prawo naturalne" [The Human Person and Natural Law]. *Roczniki Filozoficzne* 18 (1970), fasc. 2:53–59. G.: "Die menschliche Person und das Naturrecht," *VdK*, pp. 59–64.

53. "Osoba: podmiot i wspólnota" [The Person: Subject and Community]. *Roczniki Filozoficzne* 24 (1976), fasc. 2:5–39. E.: "The Person: Subject and Community," *Review of Metaphysics* 33 (December 1979): 273–301. As with *The Acting Person*, the author has reservations about the fidelity of this translation, e.g., the technical Thomistic term suppositum is often rendered "subject" (e.g., p. 274).

54. "Participation or Alienation?" *Analecta Husserliana*, vol. 6. Dodrecht, Holland: D. Reidel, 1977, pp. 61–73.

55. "The Personal Structure of Self-Determination." In *Tomasso d'Aquino nel suo VII centenario*. Rome/Naples: Congresso Internazionale, 1974. Pp. 379–90.

56. "Personalizm tomistyczny" [Thomistic Personalism]. *Znak* 13 (1961), no. 5:664–75. F.: "Le Personnalisme Thomiste," *EV*, pp. 88–101.
57. "Prawo natury" [The Law of Nature]. In the "Elementarz etyczny" series, no. 7. *Tygodnik Powszechny* 11 (1957), no. 28:7. F.: "La loi naturelle," *EV*, pp. 123–26. G.: "Das Gesetz der Natur," *EzL*, pp. 93–98.
58. "Problem bezinteresowności" [The Problem of Disinterestedness]. In the "Elementarz etyczny" series, no. 10. *Tygodnik Powszechny* 11 (1957), no. 34:7. F.: "Le problème du désintéressement," *EV*, pp. 131–33. G.: "Das Problem der Uneigennützigkeit," *EzL*, pp. 106–10.
59. "Problem doświadczenia w etyce" [The Problem of Experience in Ethics]. *Roczniki Filozoficzne* 17 (1969), fasc. 2:5–24. G.: "Das Problem der Erfahrung in der Ethik." In *W 700-leci śmierci św. Tomasza z Akwinu. Próba uwspółczesnienia jego filozofii* [On the 700th Anniversary of the Death of St. Thomas Aquinas: An Effort Towards Making His Philosophy Contemporary]. Ed. Stanisław Kamiński. Lublin, 1976, pp. 265–88. The author's lack of access to both of the previously cited works prevented him from comparing whether, in fact, they might be essentially the same work in translation.
60. "Problem etyki naukowej" [The Problem of a Scientific Ethic]. In the "Elementarz etyczny" series, no. 2. *Tygodnik Powszechny* 11 (1957), no. 10:3. F.: "Le problème de l'éthique scientifique," *EV*, pp. 107–11. G.: "Das Problem der wissenschaftlichen Ethik," *EzL*, pp. 67–72.
61. "Problem oderwania przeżycia od aktu w etyce na tle poglądów Kanti e Schelera" [The Problem of Separating Experience from the Act in the Ethics of Kant and Scheler]. *Roczniki Filozoficzne* 5 (1955–57), fasc. 3:113–40. G.: "Das Problem der Trennung von Erlebnis und Akt in der Ethik im Lichte der Anschauungen Kants und Schelers," *PG*, pp. 199–229.
62. "Problem prawdy i miłosierdzia" [The Problem of Truth and Mercy]. In the "Elementarz etyczny" series, no. 9. *Tygodnik Powszechny* 11 (1957), no. 33:11. F.: "Le problème de la vérité et de la miséricorde," *EV*, pp. 129–31. G.: "Das Problem von Wahrheit und Barmherzigkeit," *EzL*, pp. 103–6.
63. "Problem teorii moralności" [The Problem of the Theory of Morality]. In *W nurcie zagadnień posoborowych* [In the Current of Postconciliar Considerations], vol. 3. Ed. Bohdan Bejze. Warsaw, 1969, 217–49. E.: "The Problem of the Theory of Morality," in Stanisław Kaminski et al., eds., *Theory of Being to Understand Reality* (Lublin: TNKUL, 1980), pp. 163–91.
64. "Problem walki" [The Problem of Struggle]. In the "Elementarz etyczny" series, no. 19. *Tygodnik Powszechny* 12 (1958), no. 3:7. F.: "Le problème de la lutte," *EV*, pp. 152–55. G.: "Das Problem des Kampfes," *EzL*, pp. 142–47.
65. "Il problema del costituirsi della cultura attraverso la 'praxis' humana." *Rivista di Filosofia Neo-Scolastica* 69 (1977), fasc. 3:513–24.
66. "Realizm w etyce" [Realism in Ethics]. In the "Elementarz etyczny"

series, no. 4. *Tygodnik Powszechny* 11 (1957), no. 12:7. F.: "Le ré-
alisme en éthique," *EV*, pp. 114–16. G.: "Über den Realismus in der
Ethik," *EzL*, pp. 77–81.
67. "Słowo koncowe" [Closing Remarks].

(Remarks concluding a special
issue of *Analecta Cracoviensia* that grew out of a colloquium at the
Catholic University of Lublin, December 16, 1970, about Wojtyła's
Osoba i czyn). *Analecta Cracoviensia* 5/6 (1973–74): 243–63. See entry 78.
68. "Sprawiedliwość a miłość" [Justice and Love]. In the "Elementarz
etyczny" series, no. 18. *Tygodnik Powszechny* 12 (1958), no. 2:7. F.:
"Justice et amour," *EV*, pp. 149–52. G.: "Gerechtigkeit und Liebe,"
EzL, pp. 137–42.
69. "Stosunek do przyjemności" [The Relationship to Pleasure]. In the
"Elementarz etyczny" series, no. 12. *Tygodnik Powszechny* 11 (1957),
no. 38:7. F.: "Le rapport au plaisir," *EV*, pp. 135–37. G.: "Über die
Beziehung zur Annehmlichkeit," *EzL*, pp. 113–17.
70. "Subjectivity and the Irreducible in Man." *Analecta Husserliana* series, vol. 7. Dodrecht, Holland: D. Reidel, 1978, pp. 107–14.
71. "System etyczny Maksa Schelera jako środek do opracowania etyki
chrześcijańskiej" [The Ethical System of Max Scheler as a Means for
Constructing a Christian Ethic]. *Polonia Sacra*, year 6, fasc. 2/4 (1953–
54): 143–61.
72. "Teoria e prassi nella filosofia della persona umana," *Sapienza* 29
(1976), no. 4:377–84.
73. "W poczuciu odpowiedzialności" [On the Experience of Responsi-
bility]. *Kierunki* 11 (1966), no. 20:3. G.: "Im Bewußtsein der Ver-
antwortung," *VdK*, pp. 129–35.
74. "W poszukiwaniu podstaw perfekcjoryzmu w etyce" [In Search of
the Foundations of Perfectionism in Ethics]. *Roczniki Filozoficzne* 5
(1955–57), fasc. 4:303–17. G.: "Auf der Suche nach den Grundlagen
des Perfektiorismus in der Ethik," *PG*, pp. 309–26.
75. "Wartości" [Values]. In the "Elementarz etyczny" series, no. 13. *Tygodnik Powszechny* 11 (1957), no. 39:11. F.: "Les valeurs," *EV*, pp.
137–39. G.: "Über die Werte," *EzL*, pp. 117–20.
76. "Widzenie Boga" [The Vision of God]. In the "Elementarz etyczny"
series, no. 16. *Tygodnik Powszechny* 11 (1957), no. 43:7. F.: "La vision de Dieu," *EV*, pp. 144–46. G.: "Über das Schauen Gottes," *EzL*,
pp. 127–31.
77. "Właściwa interpretacja nauki o szczęściu" [The Proper Interpretation of the Teaching on Happiness]. In the "Elementarz etyczny" series, no. 11. *Tygodnik Powszechny* 11 (1957), no. 36:11. F.: "La
véritable interprétation de la doctrine du bonheur," *EV*, pp. 133–35.
G.: "Über die richtige Auslegung der Lehr vom Glück," *EzL*, pp.
110–13.
78. "Wypowiedź wstępna w czasie dyskusji nad 'Osobą i czynem' w Ka-
tolickim Uniwersytecie Lubelskim dnia 16.XII.1970" [Opening Remarks in the Course of a Discussion about *Osoba i czyn* at the Catholic

University of Lublin, December 16, 1970]. (See also entry 67.) *Analecta Cracoviensia,* 5/6 (1973–74): 53–55. KUL organized a colloquium December 16, 1970, on Wojtyła's *Osoba i czyn.* The discussions in the colloquium were subsequently published in *Analecta Cracoviensia,* 5/ 6 (1973–74). "Opening Remarks" (made by Wojtyła at the colloquium): reasons—philosophical, academic, theological—contributing to his writing of *Osoba i czyn;* he envisions the colloquium as contributing to the further development of his thought on the person and act. "Closing Remarks" represents a subsequent written reflection by Wojtyła both on the presentations at the December 16 colloquium and on those offered later in written form: whether and how *Osoba i czyn* can be deemed to have a philosophical character; whether the concept of person developed in the book corresponds to the reality of the person; what practical significance(s) and import does the notion of person developed in the book have?

79. "Zagadnienie woli w analizie aktu etycznego" [The Matter of the Will in the Analysis of the Ethical Act]. *Roczniki Filozoficzne* 5 (1955–57), fasc. 1:111–35. **G.**: "Das Problem des Willens in der Analyse des ethischen Aktes," *PG,* pp. 281–308.

80. "Znaczenie powinności" [The Significance of Obligation]. In the "Elementarz etyczny" series, no. 6. *Tygodnik Powszechny* 11 (1957), no. 16:11. **F.**: "Le sens du devoir," *EV,* pp. 119–23. **G.**: "Über die Bedeutung der Verpflichtung," *EzL,* pp. 87–93.

D. *Writings on Marriage and Family*

81. "Antropologia encykliki 'Humanae Vitae'" [The Anthropology of the Encyclical "Humanae Vitae"]. *Analecta Cracoviensia* 10 (1978): 9–28. **G.**: "Die antropologische Vision der Enzyklika 'Humanae Vitae,'" *VdK,* pp. 177–202. Italian: "La visione antropologica della 'Humanae Vitae,'" *Lateranum* 44 (1978), no. 1:125–45.

82. *Fruitful and Responsible Love.* Crossroad Books. New York: Seabury, 1979.

83. "Instynkt, miłość, małżeństwo" [Instinct, Love, Marriage]. *Tygodnik Powszechny* 8 (1952), no. 42:1–2, 11. **F.**: "Instinct, amour, mariage," *EV,* pp. 31–45. **G.**: "Instinkt, Liebe und Ehe," *EzL,* pp. 19–42.

84. *Miłość i odpowiedzialność. Studium etyczne* [Love and Responsibility: An Ethical Study]. Three Polish editions: 1st, Lublin: TNKUL, 1960; 2d, rev., enl.: Kraków: Znak, 1962; 3d, London: Veritas, 1965. **E.**: *Love and Responsibility.* Trans. H. T. Willetts. New York: Farrar, Straus, Giroux, 1981 (follows 2d and 3d eds.).

85. "Myśli o małżeństwie" [Thoughts on Marriage]. *Znak* 9 (1957), no. 7:595–604. **F.**: "Réflexions sur le mariage," *EV,* pp. 56–67. **G.**: "Gedanken über die Ehe," *EzL,* pp. 43–61. The German translation is missing approximately one and one-half paragraphs at the very beginning of the article, present in the original and in the French translation.

86. "Nauka encyckliki 'Humanae Vitae' o miłości: analiza tekstu" [The Teaching of the Encyclical "Humanae Vitae" on Love: An Analysis of the Text]. *Analecta Cracoviensia* 1 (1969), 341–56. *Humanae Vitae* contains a personalistic vision of marital love that is complementary to the vision of *Gaudium et Spes*; God's love is both "creative" and "exemplary"; man's love should also mirror God as Love and as Father; conjugal love that is human, total, faithful, exclusive, and fruitful does mirror God as Love and as Father; contraception is incompatible with the notion of "conscious parenthood," and each represents a viewpoint toward the parental vocation that is opposed to the other; the meaning of the conjugal act.

87. "O znaczeniu miłości oblubieńczej" [On the Significance of Spousal Love]. *Roczniki Filozoficzne* 22 (1974), fasc. 2:162–74. This article is a response to K. Meisnner's "The Right to the Person: The Problem of the Ethics of Sexual Life." In this article, Wojtyła examines whence the right to self-giving in the marital *communio* and in the conjugal acts of married persons derives; it does not imply "'a certain resignation from one's own *sui juris*'"; self-donation in the *communio personarum* of marriage derives from the very ontological constitution of the person as created by God.

88. "Problem 'uświadomienia' z punktu widzenia teologii" [The Problem of Sexual Education from the Viewpoint of Theology]. *Ateneum Kapłańskie*, year 54, vol. 64, fasc. 1 (1962): 1–5. G.: "Das Problem der 'Aufklärung,'" *VdK*, pp. 85–92.

89. "Promieniowani ojcostwa" [The Radiance of Fatherhood] (Drama). *Znak* 31 (1979), no. 11. E.: "The Radiation of Fatherhood," in K. Wojtyła, *The Collected Plays and Writings on Theater*, trans. Bolesław Taborski (Berkeley: University of California Press, 1987), pp. 335–64.

90. "Propedeutyka Sakramentu Małżeństwa" [Propaeudeutic of the Sacrament of Matrimony]. *Ateneum Kapłańskie*, year 50, vol. 56, fasc. 1 (1958): 20–33. Deficiencies in some modern philosophical anthropologies, which treat man as an individual egoist pursuing his own subjective good; incompatibility of such a notion with a Christian view of man as a social being joining with others in bonds based on objective common goods; implications for marriage; the Christian vision of the person in the marital and sexual sphere; marriage as sharing in the work of creation, redemption, and sanctification; love as virtue in marriage corresponding to the dignity of the person.

91. "Propedeutyka Sakramentu Malzenstwa" [Propaedeutic of the Sacrament of Matrimony]. In *Rola kobiety w Kościele* [The Role of Woman in the Church], "Wykłady i Przemówienia" series, no. 42. Lublin: TNKUL, 1958, pp. 87–92. Marriage preparation; the theological foundations of marriage; marriage preparation must take into account three aspects: the personal, the social, and the supernatural; marriage as sharing in the work of redemption; contemporary problems affecting young married couples.

92. "Przed sklepem jubilera. Medytacja o Sakramencie Małżeństwa

przechodząca chwilami w dramat" [Before the Jeweler's Shop: A Meditation on the Sacrament of Matrimony, Passing on Occasion into a Drama]. *Znak* 12 (1960), no. 12:1564–1607. E.: *The Jeweler's Shop: A Meditation on the Sacrament of Matrimony, Passing on Occasion into a Drama*, trans. Bolesław Taborski. New York: Random House, 1980; "The Jeweler's Shop," in K. Wojtyła, *Collected Plays and Writings on Theater*, trans. Bolesław Taborski (Berkeley: University of California Press, 1987), pp. 277–322.

93. "Religijne przeżywani czystości" [The Religious Experience of Chastity]. *Tygodnik Powszechny* 9 (1953), no. 6:1–2. F.: "L'expérience religieuse de la pureté," *EV*, pp. 46–55.

94. "Rodzicielstwo a communio personarum" [Parenthood and the Communio Personarum]. *Ateneum Kapłańskie*, year 67, vol. 84, fasc. 1 (1975): 17–31. G.: "Elternschaft und die Communio Personarum," *VdK*, pp. 111–28.

95. "Rodzina jako communio personarum" [The Family as a Communio Personarum]. *Ateneum Kapłańskie*, year 66, vol. 83, fasc. 3 (1974): 347–61. G.: "Familie als Communio Personarum," *VdK*, pp. 93–109.

96. "Rozważania o ojcostwie" [Considerations on Fatherhood] (Drama). *Znak* 16 (1964), no. 5:610–13. E.: "Considerations on Fatherhood," in K. Wojtyła, *Collected Plays and Writings on Theater*, trans. Bolesław Taborski (Berkeley: University of California Press, 1987), pp. 365–68.

97. "Rozważania pastoralne o rodzinie" [Pastoral Considerations on the Family]. *Roczniki Nauk Społecznych* 3 (1975): 59–76. The apostolate of the family, understood as the work of sanctification of the spouses and the family, understood in the light of Vatican II; marriage as sacramental participation in Christ's saving work; how marriage carries on that saving work through the spouses' and family's participation in the *triplex munus Christi*—priest, prophet, and king; the *triplex munus Christi* and the *communio personarum* of marriage; marriage and the task of the consecration of the world.

98. "La verità dell'enciclica 'Humanae Vitae.'" *L'Osservatore Romano* 109 (January 5, 1969): 1, 2. G.: "Die Wahrheit der Enzyklika 'Humanae Vitae,'" *VdK*, pp. 203–15.

99. "Wychowani miłości (o małżeństwie)" [The Education of Love: On Marriage]. *Tygodnik Powszechny* 14 (1960), no. 21:1. F.: "L'éducation à l'amour," *EV*, pp. 163–68.

100. "Zagadnienie katolickiej etyki seksualnej. Refleksje i postulaty" [On the Matter of Catholic Sexual Ethics: Reflections and Postulates]. *Roczniki Filozoficzne* 13 (1965), fasc. 2:5–25. Moral theology and its relation to ethics; the adequacy of the term "Catholic sexual ethics"; the material object of Catholic sexual ethics as "the relation between persons of different sex"; "naturalist" and "personalist" approaches to ethics and Wojtyła's preference for the latter; the relation of person and nature; artificial means of birth control; implications of Catholic sexual ethics for efforts to teach morality.

III. Participation by Karol Wojtyła in the Work of the Second Vatican Council

Karol Wojtyła participated in the work of the Second Vatican Council and its commissions. The following is a listing of some of Wojtyła's statements, recorded in *Acta Synodalia Sacrosancti Concilii Oecumenici Vaticani II*, published by Typis Polyglottis Vaticanis, Vatican City. The books are arranged first by session of the Council, then the volume of that session, e.g., I-2 means first session, vol. 2. The year is the date that volume was published. A brief statement of the content of the statement is supplied.

a) I-2 (1970): 314–15 (Sacraments, especially initiation)
b) I-3 (1971): 609 (Means of social communication)
c) I-4 (1971): 598–99 (Church as the Mystical Body of Christ; Mary)
d) II-3 (1972): 154–57 (The Church as People of God)
e) II-4 (1972): 340–42 (The Church and sanctification)
f) III-2 (1974): 178 79 (Mary)
g) III-2 (1974): 530–32 (Religious liberty)
h) III-2 (1974): 838–39 (Religious liberty)
i) III-3 (1974): 766–68 (Religious liberty)
j) III-4 (1974): 69–70 (Apostolate of the laity)
k) III-4 (1974): 788–89 (Apostolate of the laity)
l) III-5 (1975): 298–300 (Church in the modern world)
m) III-5 (1975): 680–83 (Amendments to schema De Ecclesia in mundo) (on behalf of Polish Episcopate)
n) III-7 (1975): 380–82 (Amendments to schema De Ecclesia in mundo) (on behalf of Polish Episcopate)
o) IV-2 (1977): 292–93 (Religious liberty)
p) IV-2 (1977): 660–63 (Church in the modern world; atheism)
q) IV-3 (1977): 242–43 (Church in the modern world; marriage and family)
r) IV-3 (1977): 349–50 (Church in the modern world; culture)

IV. Anthologies of Wojtyła's Writings

Aby Chrystus się nami posługiwał. Kraków: Wydawnictwo Znak. 1979. Broad selection of various writings, including "Elementarz etyczny" [Ethics Primer].

Collected Plays and Writings on Theater. Trans. Bolesław Taborski. Berkeley: University of California Press, 1987.

Educazione all'amore. Trans. Elżbieta Cywiak and Vladyslav [sic] Kujawski [Rome]: Edizioni Logos, 1978.

Elementarz etyczny. Lublin: TNKUL, 1983.

En Esprit et en vérité: Recueil de textes 1949–1979. Trans. Gwendoline Jarczyk. Paris: Le Centurion, 1980.
Erziehung zur Liebe: Mit einer ethischen Fibel. Stuttgart: Seewald Verlag, 1979.
Lubliner Vorlesungen. Stuttgart: Seewald, Verlag, 1981.
Poezje i dramaty [Poetry and Drama]. Kraków: Wydawnictwo Znak, 1979.
The Pope Speaks to the American Church: John Paul II's Homilies, Speeches, and Letters to Catholics in the United States. Prepared by Cambridge Center for the Study of Faith and Culture. Ed. R. Malone and S. DiGiovanni. San Francisco: Harper Collins, 1992.
Primat des Geistes: Philosophische Schriften. Stuttgart: Seewald Verlag, 1980.
Von der Königswürde des Menschen. Stuttgart: Seewald Verlag, 1980.

V. Helpful Secondary Literature

Bland, J. *The Pastoral Vision of John Paul II.* Chicago: Franciscan Herald Press, 1982.
Boniecki, Adam. *Kalendarium życia Karola Wojtyła* [A Calendar of the Life of Karol Wojtyła]. Kraków: Wydawnictwo Znak, 1983. Detailed biographical source, including a day-by-day account of Wojtyła's activities after becoming a bishop.
Buttiglione, Rocco. *Il Pensiero di Karol Wojtyła.* Milan: Jaca Book, 1982. French translation: *La Pensée de Karol Wojtyła.* Trans. H. Louette and J-M. Salamito. Paris: Communio/Fayard, 1984. One of the best comprehensive treatments of Karol Wojtyła's thought.
Gramatowski, Wiktor, and Zofia Wilińska. *Karol Wojtyła w świetle publikacji/Karol Wojtyła negli scritti: Bibliografia* [Karol Wojtyła in the Light of His Writings: A Bibliography]. Vatican City: Libreria Editrice Vaticana, 1980. The standard bibliography of Wojtyła, listing both Wojtyła's pre-papal writings and writings about Wojtyła during the same period. Entries are in Polish and Italian.
Grondelski, John. "Fruitfulness as an Essential Dimension of Acts of Conjugal Love: An Interpretative Study of the Pre-Pontifical Thought of John Paul II." Ph.D. Diss.: Fordham University, 1985. Available through University Microfilms International, Ann Arbor, MI, #86-12858.
——. "The Social Thought of Karol Wojtyła/Pope John Paul II: A Bibliographical Essay. *Social Thought* 13 (Spring/Summer 1987), nos. 2/3:151–67.
Lawler, Ronald. *The Christian Personalism of Pope John Paul II.* Chicago: Franciscan Herald Press, 1982.
Lestapis, Joseph de. "A Summary of Karol Wojtyła's *Love and Responsibility.*" In *Christian Married Love,* pp. 101–32. Ed. Raymond Dennehy. San Francisco: Ignatius, 1981.

Maliński, Mieczysław. *Pope John Paul II: The Life of Karol Wojtyła.* Image Books. Garden City, NY: Doubleday, 1982.

Mazur and Kaczyński. "Bibliografia di Karol Wojtyła." *Angelicum* 56 (1979): 73–80.

Nir, Roman. "Bibliografia prac Karola Kardynała Wojtyła Papieża Jana Pawła II za lata 1949–1978" [A Bibliography of the Works of Karol Cardinal Wojtyła/Pope John Paul II for the Years 1949–1978]. Mimeograph. Orchard Lake, Michigan: Pope John Paul II Center/Orchard Lake Schools, 1979.

Olejnik, Stanisław. "Karol Wojtyła, théologien éminent, contemporain, polonais." *Collectanea Theologica* 50 (1980), special fasc.: 11–33.

Półtawski, Andrzej. "Person and Family in the Thought of Karol Wojtyła." In *The Family in the Modern World,* pp. 53–57. Ed. Carl Anderson and William Gribbin. Washington, D.C.: American Family Institute, 1982.

Schall, J. *The Church, the State, and Society in the Thought of John Paul II.* Chicago: Franciscan Herald Press, 1982.

Seifert, Josef. "Karol Cardinal Wojtyła (Pope John Paul II) as Philosopher and the Cracow/Lublin School of Philosophy." *Aletheia* 2 (1981): 130–99.

Ślipko, Tadeusz. "Le développement de la pensée éthique du Cardinal Karol Wojtyła." *Collectanea Theologica* 50 (1980), special fasc.: 61–87.

Styczeń, Tadeusz. "Karol Wojtyła: Philosoph der Freiheit im Dienst der Liebe." In *Erziehung zur Liebe: Mit einer ethischen Fibel,* pp. 155–74. Stuttgart: Seewald Verlag, 1980.

Wilder, Alfred. "Community of Persons in the Thought of Karol Wojtyła." *Angelicum* 56 (1979): 211–44.

Williams, George H. *The Contours of Church and State in the Thought of John Paul II.* Waco, TX: Baylor University Press, 1983.

———. *The Law of Nations and the Book of Nature.* Collegeville, MN: St. John's University Press, 1985.

———. *The Mind of John Paul II: Origins of His Thought and Action.* New York: Seabury, 1981. This is the most complete global introduction to Wojtyła's thought in English.

Wolicka, Elżbieta. "Participation in Community: Wojtyła's Social Anthropology." Trans. Alice Manterys. *Communio* 8 (Summer 1981): 108–18.

Woznicki, Andrew. *A Christian Humanism: Karol Wojtyła's Existential Personalism.* New Britain, CT: Mariel, 1980. Brief but solid exposition of the general lines of Wojtyła's thought.

———. *Being and Order.* New York: P. Lang, 1989.

Index

act, human: *actus humanus (czyn)*,
41n; call to, 89; directed by will,
52–53; existential, 54. *See also*
action
Act and Lived Experience, 42
Acting Person, The: bracketing technique, 121; concluding supplement,
122; consciousness, high point of,
118; difficulty of, 62; English edition, 58–60; ideas, refinement of,
42; influences on, 36; intentionality,
denial of, 90; metaphysics in, 65;
morality, foundation of, 33; phenomenology in, 66; philosophical
anthropology, inquiry into, 34;
prefaces, two, 63; publication of,
31; realism in, 69; reflexive consciousness, 104; self-knowledge,
emphasis of, 104
action, human (*actus humanus*), 30;
anthropological foundation, 87; ba
sis and source of, 66; call to proper
by humans, 119; consummate, 119;
decisive center of, 67; distinction
between acting and being acted
upon, 78, 82; effects of, 86, 89;
ethical, 45, 54, 89; experience, role
of, 54; individual experience of, 74;
integration of, 77; "man-acts," 66,
78n, 82; moral, 144; personalistic
value of, 87–88; realistic basis of,
139; revealing the person, 66; true
nature of, 119; as vehicle to responsible freedom, 77; willed, 45;
Wojtyła's interest in and description
of, 40
Adam: Chance Interlocutor, 12, 14,
17, 19–29; inner and outer, 22, 25,
27; querulous, 95, 120
'*adam*, 99–100
agency, 46, 76, 81, 126
Albert, Brother. *See* Chmielowski
Andrew, 13–14
Anna, 13–19

anthropology, 19, 30–31, 44, 46, 49,
55, 65, 87, 90, 98, 108, 112, 116,
121;*Acting Person* as inquiry into,
34, 87; Christian, 108; definition
of, 31; of the person, 65; philosophical, 30; restrictions of term,
31; Wojtyła's expression of, 31;
Wojtyła's place within, 35
Aquinas. *See* Thomas, Saint
Aristotelian-Thomistic theory, 42, 64
Aristotle, 34, 46, 48, 50, 51
art: of serving God, 12; social responsibility of, 8; subjectivism in, 8, 9;
Wojtyła's renunciation of, 12
artistic creation, true nature of, 8
Augustine, Saint, 34, 51, 54, 87

baptism, 27
Bednarski, Feliks, 59
being: analogical character of real, 55;
as existential act, 68; metaphysics
of, 58, 65; striving for perfection
and truth, 52
biblical history, plays as dramatic expression of, 2
Blondel, Maurice, 35
body, 101, 103, 107
Bonaventure, Saint, 34, 54
boundary experience, 106
bracketing, 67–68, 121
Buber, Martin, 36

catharsis of meaning, 5
causation, lived, 127–28
cause: causal originator, 49, 68; lived
experience of, 127
Centesimus Annus, 97n, 116, 123
Child, 28
children, love requires us to become
as, 19, 27
Chmielowski, Adam, 8
Christ: as citizen, 118; at the center,
1, 109, 146; Bridegroom, 12, 14,
28–29; calls each acting person,
120, 138; the new Adam, 117;

165